LAST DAY OF THE YEAR

Selected Poems

LAST DAY OF THE YEAR

Selected Poems

MICHAEL KRÜGER

Edited by
Stanley Moss

Translations by
Karen Leeder and Richard Dove

The Sheep Meadow Press
Rhinebeck, NY

The German texts in this selection were originally published in Germany by Suhrkamp Verlag, Residenz Verlag, and Carl Hanser Verlag in the following volumes:

Diderots Katze © 1978 by Carl Hanser Verlag
Nachts, unter Bäumen © 1996 by Residenz Verlag
Kurz vor dem Gewitter © 2003 by Suhrkamp Verlag
Unter freiem Himmel © 2007 by Suhrkamp Verlag
Ins Reine © 2010 by Suhrkamp Verlag
Umstellung der Zeit © 2013 by Suhrkamp Verlag

English Translations from *Diderot's Cat* and *At Night, beneath Trees* by Richard Dove © 1990, 1998

English Translations from *Kurz vor dem Gewitter, Unter freiem Himmel, Ins Reine,* and *Umstellung der Zeit* by Karen Leeder © 2003, 2007, 2010, 2013, 2014

Designed and typeset by The Sheep Meadow Press
Distributed by The University Press of New England

All inquiries and permission requests should be addressed to the publisher:

The Sheep Meadow Press
PO Box 84
Rhinebeck, NY 12572

Library of Congress Control Number: 2014947212

Contents

FROM *Shortly Before the Storm*, 2003
TRANSLATED BY Karen Leeder

FROM *UNDER AN OPEN SKY*, 2007
TRANSLATED BY KAREN LEEDER

FROM *FAIR COPY*, 2010
TRANSLATED BY KAREN LEEDER

FROM *TIME TO BE CHANGED*, 2013
TRANSLATIONS BY KAREN LEEDER

Many thanks to Naveen Kishore of Seagull Books for allowing us
to print Karen Leeder's translations from *Umstellung der Zeit*.

from *Diderot's Cat*
1990

BEFORE THE MEAL, FOUR IN THE MORNING

I've never yet eaten on my own, all myself,
she said, have never yet had the feeling of having
taken a meal independently. First there was Mother
(she said as she stood there in front of the fridge) who not only

stood at my side and wielded my spoon, determining
how and what and how much I should eat, but who also
was there in the food itself. I only ate to give
pleasure to Mother. She wasn't just there in the food, in

the dishes, but—increasingly—was the food itself.
My mother, she said—standing there in front of the open
fridge in a nightdress, freezing—was, as it were, my
daily bread. Which explains how thin she is, so she

claimed, her total inability to keep food down;
as well as her total lack of interest in certain foods.
In restaurants, for instance, the feeling of being in a
museum, the feeling of standing entirely outside

the natural order: her greed in restaurants, the manic wish
to order everything coupled with the grim awareness
that she could not even begin to pick at a single
thing. Her exultation when faced with rotten meals in

inns: had I noticed? I had no intention
of being drawn. Had I been forcibly struck as well
by the desperate loneliness of diners, especially
of fat ones, throughout the whole eating process, by their

attempts to fill themselves to the brim, attempts
that are doomed? The inability to put
the mess of dishes in apple-pie order reminded her
of museums too: greed, she went on, is due to a

rage for order or, rather, to a quite unappeasable
rage for order. The wide-open eyes are a pointer here:
eyes in search of a system which they, of course, will not
find. I, for example, just cannot eat with my eyes

4

closed, she said: the notion of not being able to see
what I'm eating brings on attacks of vertigo, peri-
stalsis cuts out automatically, even if I've
seen the waiter bringing the meal, that he's really

brought it. She was ice-cold. I: You have got very thin
of late. She: In critical situations, I always,
now, put on weight; the very presence of
others makes me swell up. They are all attempting un-

consciously to gorge me; surrendering, losing
weight would be out of the question in such situations;
at such times I feel unfortified. (And years ago?) I'd
have slimmed down at once, would (so to speak) have dispersed myself;

everything used to flow out of me—quite noticeably
I could literally see how everything flowed away
out of me. In critical situations, she used,
at once, to become as thin as a rake. Like now,

I said. Suddenly it was light outside.
The fridge was open, as before; it was very cold. You're cold,
I said. She replied: the whole complex business of eating,
the mumbojumbo of eating, the thrills that it used

to give me now, in retrospect, send a shiver
down my spine; I stole into the kitchen
in order to learn how to eat. Admittedly, that sounds rather
odd. Utopia is keeping one's weight

when the going gets rough. I'd like to keep mine
when the going gets rough, and that's why I'm here.
I want to surrender nothing and to assimilate
nothing; I want to be impregnable and very round.

That is one's only hope, she maintained, trembling
with cold. A round glass body in which one can
watch the process of digestion and that of
decomposition, excretion, without the body

altering: I'm well on the way to achieving that state.
I can't understand why such things hold so little interest
for people. Why, she asked, has it all been forgotten?
I put all the hotplates on and began with the preparations.

Diderot, I said, getting down to peeling potatoes—
something in Diderot—craved potatoes on his deathbed, a
truly polemical wish in the history of civilization.

(for Fred Oberhauser)

POSTLIMINARY POEM

The signs are speaking
a different language:

they've every right to.
We thought that their
ambiguity
was as safe as houses,

and now are offended,
tight-lipped. Once again

we're sitting there stranded
in alien chairs and rooting,
resigned, in paper-filled lairs. There's
reason, no rhyme, now in many things:

rich rhymes that, several years back,
would have seemed like slips of the tongue.

ARCHAEOLOGY

1

All year long ('75) I was out
to write a political poem on

Germany; it was to be called The Unnatural
Warmth, and was intended for a friend in

California who could not make it to
Germany that year, who could not travel

through Germany in the year in question
to see for himself all the things that had changed:

the poem was to have filled the gap
between what was, then, his most recent stay

and his next, to prevent him from taking fright
when he next came, from taking the next plane back,

or from having to hurry to check his ticket
to see, for example, whether he'd landed

somewhere else. All year long I gathered
material for The Unnatural Warmth

concerning the unnatural warmth that had spread
through Germany: in the papers and journals,

in houses and flats and out on the
streets, in people's heads and in discussions

about the great cold they said had spread
in the papers and journals, and out on the

streets, and in houses and flats, and in discussions,
and in people's heads. On the first of each month

I got down to sifting through the notes
towards my meteorological poem:

the notes on the wind which, suddenly violent,
had turned against us; and on the rapidly

spreading depression and on the concomitant
change of weather; the cold sea-air from South-Western

Europe they said should have blown northeasterly;
on all the climactic fluctuations and other meteoro-

logical shocks. I was out to attempt
to describe the fear that was spreading, the fear

of the cold spell forecast and what that fear meant:
that everyone suddenly huddled together

to warm each other; and suddenly got
all wrapped up, beyond recognition almost;

that hardly anyone graced the streets;
that the few who did were glued to the sky,

interpreting cloudscapes; that, as a result
of the fear of the coldspell that had been forecast,

summer in Germany felt like December.
People are whispering as in winter, I noted, and yet

the sun is beating down hotter than ever. It was to have been
a poem on the spread of the power of meteoro-

logy and on its demonstrably incorrect forecasts.

2

At the end of the year, on 16.12.1975,
the bag with my notes was stolen at Tegel

Airport. I sat there, morose, in a hotel
in Littlehampton, on England's south coast, opposite

Europe; outside it was cold and pouring with rain.
I spent my time wondering whether, for climatic reasons,

they'd changed the course of the Gulf Stream. Un-
interruptedly, I read German papers that all arrived

appallingly late. In Germany archaeology
had been rediscovered, so I read; I thought un-

interruptedly of my poem. Blimey, can time
really pass that quickly. The archaeology of opera. The

archaeology of the cinema. My major political poem
on Germany: up the spout. I tried to imagine

gigantic excavation sites in Germany—
the Rhine-Main Region dug up completely,

and Baden-Württemberg one big black hole. The archaeology
of the Future. The year which had just passed was also judged

in terms of all sorts of archaeological
factors. A very odd business. My year,

the year of my projected poem. Oddly enough,
there were few overlaps. Regarding the climate,

all the commentaries differed from my
observations, for instance. Or take another fact

that featured in none of the retrospects: in '75
Fascism had been thirty years dead (or maybe not).

Instead a long list of dead individuals everywhere:
white-haired men and women with faces furrowed

by care. I flew back as fast as I could to Berlin
to search on the spot for my manuscripts:

the poem I'd planned would indeed fill a gap
in the market, if it did get written,

or so I thought. But, when disembarking,
a voice in me said: you'll never find your bag with the notes,

never again. It was hellish cold there in Berlin,
the ice-bound flat was especially

unbearable: muffled in pullovers, blankets, I crouched
beside the window and crossly mused

on the loss of my poem and on the curious
boom in archaeology in Germany.

THE FELONY

Didactic Poem for Brecht's 80th Birthday

We've got to make
the leaves fall faster
We'll take the risk
We've got no choice but to fell
the tree at one fell swoop
We'll take the risk
We urgently need
the earth underneath
We appreciate that
Those who hesitate ought to consider:
Lofty Nature alone
will remember what befell.
We're risking the Fall.

THE CAT IS DEAD

I found her
next to the dustbin
stiff
after a supple life.

Strange,
she was lying on her belly
with paws outstretched.

It was in this position
she'd lie in front of me
when I was prompted to read to her.

What caught her fancy
were old travel books.
She knew, for example,
by heart the true story
of Oblomov's voyage
round the world.
(As is well known,
this Czarist official
did not go ashore a single time
in the whole of the journey.)
Outlandish things
held no appeal,

I said to her
when she was keen
to slip off that night.
She frequently
treated me
like a child.

But when I actually
acted like one,
she'd instantly
bristle.

Errors, lack of attentiveness
she'd correct
with a courteous
quiver of whiskers.

Each of us
led a double life—
she at night
and I in the daytime—
which we hid from one another,
sedulously.

Only of late
did she hint that I was to
be let in on
her fur-warm life

as a reward
for patient observing.
Now she has died
in the posture of listening.

And I feel
the victim.

ERNST MEISTER IN MEMORIAM

In things
the eyes, Ernst,
prior to language.
Wherever you are
you return:
stone, threshold, house
are watching you closely.
Therefore, Ernst,
you remain alive,
always in view.

DIDEROT'S CAT
Photographed by Gabriele Lorenzer

Diderot at the window: at his side the cat—
her scaly fur in the bright window frame.

Man, the machine, he explains to her
in a toneless voice: the rudiments
of physiology, intellect,
the violent workings of nature too.

He quotes the proceedings
of the Academy of Sciences for the year 1739
where mention is made of a man
without veins, without a heart.
On page 590, he adds with a hollow laugh,
caressing the fur of his cat
not without embarrassment.

Some photographs have a longer history
than photographic history does.

The cat watches closely as a cloud
travels briskly past in the
upper third of the window, too briskly:
her reflex reaction is panic-stricken.
Diderot, ground down by thirty years' labor
towards the Encyclopédie
is speechless:
the vehement dialectician admires
the simple grammar of nervousness.

A dog's whole soul resides in its snout,
he says, an eagle's in its eye,
a mole's in its ear. Diderot wonders
whether or not he ought to continue.

Man's soul, he starts again
—and breaks off
                    (soullessly cool,
the cat is writing a treatise on the influence
of the climate on the muddy
glass);

(Diderot's watching
the revolution from the window, its gingerly
steps);
     an eccentric couple:
Diderot and the cat
in the badly cracked window-cross:
his fear of imitating her movements,
her mild polemic against his theory
of the machine.

We walk so little
work so little
and think so much, says Diderot,
that man in the end
will be nothing but head.

It's Sunday afternoon:
a good time
to remember emotions;
it's cold in Paris,
extremely quiet;
it comes home to Diderot just how hard
it is to smuggle his knowledge to safety.

Thirty years' labor towards the Encyclopédie
and still the machine's not working
the way it should. He gingerly probes
the bones, the bone structure, of his cat.

We'll prove the first barbarians,
he suddenly says, the lachrymose tone
in his voice loud and clear.
His hollow laughter laments the aging
of an illusion. The cat is contented.
Squinting, she's contemplating
the dust beside the window
and couldn't care less
that Reason knows no moderation.

Diderot admits defeat.
He glumly shuffles across to his desk
and notes down the following:

Where do I come from?
What did I used to be previously?
What is the point of my present existence?
What kind of life is awaiting me?

In what sort of frame will my fate
recreate me?
I have no answers.

He runs to the window
and—after a quick look down at the
street—begins to brood.

Only much later,
after the cat, with a mighty leap,
has freed herself
from the picture's cramping, constricting frame,
does he add serenely:

Philosophy too is instruction
in dying.

ELEGY

Bolzano. A lying in statelessness:
no password exists that could
gain me entry. Some shuffling
gets around like a rumor behind
the mountains; a history, a story
asks the way.

Air, air. Were you waiting
for me who came one day too late?
Your best blue shirt,
your light pair of trousers.
What shall I do with your hand
which can't greet me?

There's snow in your hair,
let me warm you.
Is there a picture of you?
Time has replaced
your body. A stranger,
you're my best friend.

You have to come back
to Germany, Father—
to my side where death
is not spoken about.
You're laughing? Your open mouth
casts suspicion on me. Too late.

How small you are! Though
one grows a little
after death—just as
Death is growing, this moment, in us:
a witness of stainless character
with great clout at court.

A forged passport. Quick;
your life can't be cramped
in obituaries. Two birds are keeping
watch at the border. Beneath
the black body of the clouds,
by stealth, you come back home to us.

Then, at last, earth. At last
the sand of Berlin: up here
you may finally die. You fling Death
like a cloak around your heart of ash
and set yourself free and make no reply
for every answer would be a question.

(for Helmut Otto Krüger)

FOOTNOTE

We're coming back to fetch
what remains: pillow; pillowcase; pall;
a drawing which hung unprotected
above the stove: Hermes, the Guide
of the Dead who, for the space of four years,
added spice to our meals. God has still
not been born; the clock stays hanging there;
so, in the hall, does the mirror. How
the flat grows and grows, the more it
empties and how small is Time,
brooding away in the tomb-like rooms.
All is now dark, we've
removed the lamps: everything
passes softly through us. From where
my writingdesk once was,
I try to decipher a note
on the wall: Your Anger is Love.
A footnote in the history
of vanity, still to be written.

SKÁCEL

The lateness of the hour
drove him home. Another drink,
a cigarette, a word
that will pass through the Jewish Gate
with its fluttering tongues.
Once a year someone
hangs himself, from someone
else's hand the world falls.
Neat little verses can't
outface Death, the Moravian
Master. Here in Brünn
the snow is like dust.
Your dark eyes
beneath their burning brows,
your shirt full of burrs.
Another week
and we'll see one another;
you've been dead six days.

CAHORS

Someone who's come unannounced is standing
deep in the twilight: making
the silence grow
beneath the ploughed-up clouds.
We understand him,
understand his unreasonable joy.

As though beneath trees in the winter
when the final leaf,
only moments ago the world's mirror,
spins down, spins down,
strikes the ground.

Cathedrals like trees.
Hugging the trunk like a lover,
unasked, someone's
standing there and decoding the boughs.

A LETTER FROM ROME

1

On one of the very few bright mornings
in February, thick red sand dust lay
on the window sills, doubtless
from Africa, maybe Tunisia,
dropped here in Rome by a
sensitive wind. A rare occurrence
in February which I wanted to mark.
I started to write on the three window sills
in the way one writes with a finger
on sand: a soft calligraphy
full of round forms that—some time or other—
will be destroyed by some gentle rain.

2

Some time or other. It was a poem
about the small stretch of desert within us,
about the sand which, as long as we live,
we count in our roaming hope
for knowledge, about the countless imitations,
about the uncountable repetitions.
The last line ran: My anguish
ceased, my cares blew away.
My index finger was burning but I
felt no pain: the text
had been written and no gentle rain
would ever be able to blot it out.

3

And, as you know, it rained a good deal
this February, here in this world
of crumbling stone which put
the text to the test. And us too.
The sky: a corrupt, impure source.
Nothing, however, could get me to doubt
the connection existing between the red sand,
that had flown across the benighted sea,
and the carefully copying hand
that, against the run of experience, ordered that sand.
Beaches thus come into being on which
we peacefully sit, on to which we're cast up.

20TH OCTOBER 1989

Outside my window, right before my eyes,
Orion's dog, white Sirius, is sniffing
away through the hungry branches, cool, bedewed,
suspended in infinite distance. Near things are blurred;
the radio's reedy voice: the capital
moves slowly east, into the neck of the world.
Dark horses as they are, the dreamers lose
the wager with themselves, and are relieved:
the thin ice crackles, breaks
above the words. One past, one path;
renunciation of all other paths.
And then the birds return, desires
huddle together as do clouds.
Day breaks in the room. Oblivious,
disgusted by the shop-soiled range of moods,
I try to think the whole thing through, and through:
the world appears, dismembered, in a poem.

NERO PILED LEAD ON HIS CHEST

Nero piled lead on his chest
in order to make his voice
stronger. Every word:
a scar burnt into
the dirty slate that is memory.
Others live on the interest
from silence; questions too
are a livelihood.
A nail avails
against nightly raving,
a nail that's been torn from a sepulcher.
Once I knew someone
who made insects crawl
across the empty page
of his notebook, and who—
in the tenuous shadow-script—
read his life to the end.

Richard Dove

20

from *At Night, Beneath Trees*

1998

GUIDED TOUR

What you see here is wrested out of History's jaws.
All beams are old; all doorframes too,
in which the dead used to hang, for three days.
At this table, world history was written
(the notches betray as much): here a gallows,
and there the king's head. We can only conjecture
who this woman can be, legs astraddle.
Wars were in fashion because there were still "destinies"
which had to be fulfilled. There were goals.
A sharp sword came out of his mouth, which meant
he could express himself, be understood:
language had not yet been mastered by Doubt
but was shaped by vision; no sign of an archive
of emptiness. A person at this table received
his identity from the looks of others, under duress too.
There was no chair in this room for Fear,
which is why it nestled down into the painters' fine brushes,
as you can see from these pictures: here it has survived
in a transport of color. The pictures were cleaned
when the last war ended. Although Enlightenment
virtues are still important to us, they're not
absolute. They learned, in those days, to classify birds:
those which one hears and those which one sees. Today we listen
to what the town has to tell us about time, congestion, lateness.
If you'd be so kind as to follow me, this is the way to the
exit.

LITTLE GERMAN NATIONAL ANTHEM

Just imagine we owned this house,
the friendly creaking of the stairs
and the mice behind the wainscoting.
Just imagine the shades of those
who lived here once were crowding
the table too, telling stories.
We'd be listening. Wearing their clothes,
with collars turned inside out, dyed in the
wool. And the corpulent angel
of history would be chopping onions,
shedding salty tears for us.

Just imagine we asked the brook
to leave its gravelly bed so the fish
would not have to cross the land
on its way into our pot.
Just imagine that we were sleeping
at night in these beds and that the country
covered us right up with its dreams.

Just imagine we dreamed we had to
leave the house and had no idea
where we should go.

THE PARROT

Don't talk to me of truth,
please don't, in this Museum
of Art. Ask the fly
that's turned that window into a matter
of life and death, making the dirt
dance choice arabesques. The master
has left the house, don't ask
how; the paint is still wet
on the canvas; and, inside the computer,
a short poem's waiting
for its last line.
The guests alone are lolling still
in their easy chairs: worn out, as though gagged,
by a tangled discussion.
Nothing more can be got
beyond: that is the truth.
Talk to the stones outside,
growing dreamily out of the earth,
or else to the clouds, to the rain.
No points of view though, please,
but only sacred signs. I'm
the resident parrot, my word hoard's
as small as that of my master,
whose name escapes me.
I am old.
And please, no questions! For if there were
an answer, it would be concealed
within the question. My plumage cries
out to be described
but only from outside, through the window,
so that the guests are not woken.

CARBON PAPER

In the beginning, I read, there was perhaps the cross
and, above the cross, a pallid sun,
spirited up into the sky as if by magic.
The sky has been written across. Despite
the handiwork of an alien hand,
I can still make out its long-suffering face: two snails for eyes,
and, for a mouth, a fish's skeleton.
I hazily read the unreadable love,
the deception in the language: I know, you know—
child's play for even the blind to decipher.

ADVICE

If you want to paint paradise
looking its best, don't skimp
on color. Too little
smooths everything—for example,
the ocean will look like a notional
ocean. Just paint one tear,
just paint the reflection of your face
in a drop of water,
and there is the wave,
the pebble on the ocean floor,
the shipwreck, paradise itself.
Too little color's too much
for us and we (after all) want it
to speak our language
in our pictures. We've always
understood what appears:
a house by an ocean
in a hot summer,
entirely white: as though we'd painted
in snow.

LETTER

Yesterday evening—don't
ask me why—I went into the village
church and sat down, shivering,
among the old folks
in one of the cramped pews;
I moved my lips as though I had something
to contribute. It was dead easy.
As soon as the first prayer was over
(we also prayed for you), the mask
of Goodness grew over my face.
Up front, not demanding a solution,
the old priest was pecking listlessly
around in the gospel, like some black bird,
but he didn't appear to find anything
that could have graced us.
No saving thread, no consolation.
One hour and everything was over.
Outside, an unexpectedly bright light
played on the lake, and a wind sprang up—
letting me see the under-
side of the leaves.

SERVICE STATION

I'm just repeating the sentences
of those who've spoken before me—public servants, middle
managers, white-collar workers, ordinary mortals.
They all say more or less the same:
my car is sputtering, vibrating wildly,
will not speed up when I put my foot down.
Blindly I grope for words
as though they were a tool. If something is missing,
I am all eyes. I can't help
my language—it's there and has got to be
used or else it will soon be rusty.
I say to my wife: the food tastes fine.
Or else: I love you. Sometimes I fling
myself into the arms of words, but that's
bad for business. Take yesterday:
a poet was here, a real old-timer—
pure gibberish. His spark plugs were all
clogged up with soot, that's all that was wrong,
but he couldn't describe it, too sad.
It is a mistake to believe, he said,
but by then I was under the hood.

AFTERNOON

Books by the window, thinned by the sun,
behind your back the heavy breathing of the pages:
rising and falling, rising and falling . . .
Apart from novels, poems, each houses
a hidden language, a couple of words
in an arid paper nest; the rest
is lumpy grammar.
At times there's a sentence that's all divine.
When questioned, put on the spot, under pressure,
they, none of them, own up to having heard it.

A friend returns, brings the world
indoors—the mountain that, burning, slid into the ocean,
the birdcalls, the snail's trail left by Doubt.
He tells you of regions like empty classrooms
(all knowledge driven out with a pitchfork).
Hey, come on, you're exaggerating!
But he's already turned to a new page,
is pointing to a watermark, the labyrinth
of a finger from way back, two thumbwidths
from the original.

Salts proliferate on the pages, spawning trees
on whose parched branches lies are thriving.
Have no expectations. Count letters, syllables,
till a word arises which inspires your trust.
That word will get you back into the sentence.

COMMEMORATIVE SHEET FOR GÜNTER EICH

Out in the garden stand two shoes,
not a pair, out of breath
after traveling far.
They look both old and bold
in the dewy grass of dawn.
One is squeaking in prose,
the other in stumbling verse.
We have invented roads for ourselves
which no man ever set foot upon . . .
It's pretty bombastic,
not all that credible and, after all:
a good shoe doesn't betray the path
it has taken,
a good shoe stays silent.
I really could chuck them away
but leave them. Almost noon
they've upped and left.

PS

for Marianne and Peter

Yesterday there were stewed apples made of fruit from Tutzing,
fruit which we had (as it were) known from birth:
we had already admired the blossom, its bright
shriek in spring, and later the tiny green balls
and the way the grass turned white in the wake of the storm.
We watched as the apples grew bigger,
got covered with stains but still stayed green,
stayed greenish-black. Back in the summer we wondered
how they'd taste in the fall,
and when the first ones lay in the grass, green set off by green,
we threw them across the garden for the dogs to chase,
for Billie and Ella. For many years now
we've been counting on the apples from the garden in Tutzing.
While the world (whatever that is) demands
we assume the relativity of all forms of knowledge,
while we're left with understanding, unable to see our way
through anything anymore, the apple tree's lesson is simple:
it gets repeated year after year in an old-fashioned manner
regardless of what people think of each other,
and shows a certitude that Reason can only dream of.
Shortly after the frost—the front had moved to the west—
we picked the apples, which now looked ancient,
diseased and decrepit, as they ought to.
They tasted exceptionally good, somewhat sour,
and after the first bite we had to look back.
Then yesterday came what was left over, stewed.
While eating the forbidden we had a lengthy discussion
about the fact that we have to assume a reality
to which to react, one way or another.
I can't say we were out of the garden.

LETTER TO A CHILD
for Simon

Thank you warmly for your letter.
The fresh green of the envelope pleased me—
I'm going to keep it, although I too wish to part with
things. I'll have to die when this place is full.
Your envelope's attached to the lamp:
it's darker now, the paper is no longer white,
and your handwriting's gleaming: I'll never again
forget my name or address. There's too much
of everything—we've got to learn
to throw things away. To question is: what?
Tears come to my eyes when I pass the garbage can
in the morning. Yesterday, beneath coffee grounds
and potato peel, a whole coat was lying there, one sleeve hang-
ing over the edge, one button short.
A proper coat, a coat people wear.
Everything turns into history, trash, if a button's missing—
a laughable button made of plastic.
The massive Soviet Union has just fallen
apart, and nobody knows what the parts are called,
but each part has a name. Fine names
that make the newscaster on TV—the man
with the round face—stutter. All men are brothers now,
but otherwise nothing has changed.
I'm sorry, there's too much *now*,
too little *yesterday* and *tomorrow* in this letter; all's
gathered up in this *now*, this point
which closes something. I'm not sure if I can muster
a lion. ("Lion" is spelled with an "i," by the way—
regards to your teacher.) At any rate,
the lion that lives here is looking for another apartment.
It brings me the mail, from time to time, in its dripping mouth,
which means I can't work out who's the sender.
I'll only write to you in future anyway. Visit me soon,
for when you're grown up I'll already be dead.

LETTER TO DAN PAGIS

Dear friend, the enemy's disappeared.
He left behind a note, brown paper:
"You're not to remember, at any price."
At times, when I'm sitting in the chair
that you sat in and the cloud's lucent map
is laying out a worm-eaten shadow
on the road, I see the horse,
the gravedigger's house, and remember the time
we exchanged our words: my name
is Adam and this is Abel, my good-natured son;
don't let his behavior put you off.
We've booked a ticket right to the very
end of the world, can stop over as often
as we like. There'll always be a garden, a house,
a child that dreams of wind from the ocean,
of fire in the fields. It isn't good
to sit for too long . . . We used to live
in that house over there; it was a shed
for the goats. There were still many gods in those days.
And many tongues crowded desperately
around few words. No end was in sight.
And next-to-no bureaucracy. My dad, who was bright,
applied himself to reading the symptoms
because he was crazy enough to want to abolish disease.
Since he died, we've been traveling,
escorted by voice and text, our shadows.
This, dear Dan Pagis, is what we wanted to translate—
transport, word by word, to the other language.
Can it be me that's sitting in your chair?

RETURNING TO AN EMPTY HOUSE

You didn't remember to water the flowers,
and an apple's dry mummy is stiff in the
ashtray, a mournful brown wreck in a field
of ash. There are hairs all round too, as if some
poor creature had met a foul end. On the window sill
flies, their legs in the air, and a spider which moves
away like a dead weight when I touch it.
It's all spilt milk, with a coating of dust.
No image. That corpse they found in the Alps, 4,000
years old, an image of man, still had hair
when they sighted it under the ice, and a smile
on its lips, the first known smile, in all
likelihood, in the brief little history
of mankind—and from it derives the whole
fine art of being human. At some point
it came apart like the cloud that's coming apart now
outside the window: not some sudden severance
but rather a gentle unraveling, a fluffy parting
with each part promising to keep
a tiny scrap of the other forever.
One part of this ancient smile is allied
with man whenever, unsure of himself,
he stumbles over a threshold, the other
has grown into an inordinate laugh that no
longer fits into any face. Since that time, a smile's
been hiding in every guffaw, and vice versa too—
the law holds true in this empty house.
Everything's turning up again, coming back to light,
now the snow is melting, a tooth
for a tooth. And even the handful of pitiful words
which are still straightforwardly ours, and which
we squirreled away till spring so we'd find
a rhyme for meadows and sheep and light's
rite, are becoming apparent, sodden like
dog dung and forming a lusterless wreath round themselves,
from which they then shyly arise: grace,
return. All things are on hand, all things,
including departure, demise; it's just that they don't
look the same when someone suddenly pulls
away the blanket of dross and dream, releasing a smile

which ascends like a bird alarmed in its sleep.
The tempest raised a veil of purest white . . .
The earth, sick unto death, sweats out its dead
and stops the future becoming the future.
Plates in the sink. Dried coffee grounds
are narrating stories in my favor with both beginnings
and endings as though I'd only a past.
No sleep between the lines, no respite,
no death which kills us with sharp-edged eyes,
I've got to sit down, my head is swimming
with all the invocations booming out of this silence,
out of the silence of silence, out of the navel of language
down under the snow. Things are appearing
outside the house: stones, ferns, the brown grass
and, there in their midst, old forgotten tracks that
showed the way long before the road did, the much-traveled
road. And behind lies the wood which barely harbors
the roe deer's bounding shadows until
they're flooded by darkness. And no
trails, so all is in order in this empty
house. You've forgotten, lost to whatever, to turn
the computer off too: I can see its glassy
emerald eye, the other light. It now knows music
back to front, can simulate every single note
with its AAA1 memory. All things are
on hand. All things fit easily onto a chip
the size of a thumbnail—words and notes,
the whole of history, and when the eye's burning
all things are with us, simultaneous,
with or without us. It all works without us,
nobody's looking for us now. Each delicate smile
and each guffaw from time out of mind
has access to me. All things allow us
to share in them, and we share in all.
The whispering tissue of traces which go to make
consciousness, history, a tenuous
present, is centerd on one point,
the point of irreversible beauty,
which now is slowly fading. When was I
last in this house?
I move from photo to photo; all strangers.
One was a thinker, I recognize him:

there's death in his eyes, the death which loved him
from cradle to grave. They're all hanging here to be
forgotten. Look, there's the idiot, the family idiot,
destroyer of books: his folks couldn't work out
whether he was in the grips of madness
or just adept at the language of madness;
there's the dear lived-in face he was wont to
press to the ground to hear the moles
at work. Human beings become more mournful
the longer they hang here behind cobwebs, glass.
They look like children grown old overnight,
like children without a future. And then
these newspapers, printed nature. History
is over, it's said, there's nothing to
look forward to. We've got to live on
what we have and are, no new growth is in the cards,
no new installment of dreams. And no art.
So that was it: from the ban on incest
right down to free market economics we swept
the board. With skirts getting longer and shorter by turns,
and somewhere along the way the invention of perspective,
the twelve-tone series, the cordless phone.
Of course at some point the king's head had to
roll, and time was ripe at another juncture
for universal suffrage. We can still recall
the circling finger in the sand, and chalk,
and pencil, and typewriter. And the historians
will hit upon whether Landor wrote
with his right or his left hand. History will win
at the end of history—the history of the
handkerchief that wiped tears for good
from the face of the earth. And everything just
in our heads, in which several wires are better
or differently linked than in those of dogs.
I envy dogs. I'd like to embrace
every horse. Every bird turns my head, every crow.
So now we are to take our leave from this
empty house, from these lofty looks,
these lordly gestures, our humble words,
an impossible present. Having struggled
up from our squatting position we walked a few years erect,
straight ahead, invented the gods and quickly

forgot them again, and now it's all over.
A drag mark, transparent, is running through
the house, across paper, like that made by snails.
And yet . . . I am reaching no conclusion, no
beginning. Not much mail. One fellow wants money,
another's sent poems. One is a tactful description of
an empty house in which you can walk from room to room
without let or hindrance, wall or door.
The house is empty. A good sort of poem
in free verse, so useless and so detestably
true.

THE DAY AFTER

In fact, what I aimed to do today (Monday)
was get to write a love poem of sorts,
an unassuming piece on a couple
I kept my eyes on yesterday
in a pub (called Kosta). I wasn't out
à la Dante, "to imitate God's language,"
nor to resort to irony, but just to describe
the nexus of power, desire, and knowledge,
as revealed to yours truly, your typical
nervous observer: in snatches of speech,
looks, attitudes, in the manner in which
the man ordered more wine, the woman smoked.
A love poem was to have emerged
which didn't breathe a word about
the steady dissolution of culture—
the thing which preoccupies me all day
because its progress cannot be checked.
Inquiring into the nature of poetry
challenges us to reflect on the state
of our existence. If I don't study
my mistakes, the mistakes made by poetry,
I'm bound to repeat them; it's no good either
invoking Freedom, which (it's said)
becomes flesh in poems, even in
their very line breaks. I had in mind
the artless utopia of a happy
meeting of bodies, unmindful of death, destruction
and catastrophe. The words, though,
refused to yield up their truth,
as though they'd no idea how perception
and knowledge are rendered into language.
This may be the reason why love
poems are so short these days,
and why their findings—if one may say this—
are foreseeable.

IN CONVERSATION

You know that I'm only a guest
in this house, a man who seeks
the shade beneath the transcendent trees,
a short-lived alliance as evening draws down.
I am the eye while the wind
is reading in the hedge, and painting
a grimace on the back of the brook
that is struggling seaward—to protect it
against the night, which has not yet struck.
Between removal and return
the salt is glittering ambivalently
in the falling sun.
You know whom I turn to:
the face which sees me,
unrecognizing. Day's
done; the watchmen are rising, white,
out of the grass and are sitting in judgment—
but always in such a way that they keep
in God's good books.

TO BE CONTINUED

The house is bristling still with the mousetraps
the last tenant set, and in the corners
stand little dishes flush with red poison—
designed to give the flies one last
fling. Black beetles are out
of it on their backs, as though
they tried their best to tread air.
The only protagonists who seem
at home are the spiders; with flimsy legs,
they're busy narrating the novel whose outcome
we're unaware of. It started, apparently,
with a murder that left a red thread
on all the walls that hold this place up.
And then the day of the victim dawned, and then came
the war. And now we live here.
Waiting for the wind which will bring
the host of words home from the empty sky.

THE BED

After you'd left
I stripped your bed.
The mattress looked
like a convict, finished.
Now, when I turn out the light,
I can't be sure any more
on which side I'm lying.
With one foot in jail
and the other in freedom,
sleep's out of the question.

LOOKING OUT INTO THE GARDEN

If only I were able to describe
the fluttering lashes of the laurel—
which rise in the gale and only fall
when the shadows take umbrage from the dark green—
in words, in words which are consonant.
Beauty is not a prerogative
of the person at the window, staring
out at the bordered paths, the well
(whose stones are making off) and the herbs
(arranged in classes, just like school);
one's privilege is the words that are crouching
restlessly in one as though inside a breathing ark,
just waiting for the rain to stop.
Some of them leave one's mouth prematurely
and fly off in horror, others stay put
inside the husk assigned to them.
We choose our language, and not the other way around,
and even eyes that soundlessly sound off
seek the right words when the time
is ripe. Yet, sometimes, when one is standing
silently by the window, watching the laurel
coquettishly yielding to the wind,
a voice which isn't one's own speaks up. Says:
fluttering lashes.

WIND

A simple universal answer
embracing both grains of sand and stars,
both God and worm. A tool, some forceps:
the instruments needed to measure the world
can only be found in the world. I'm standing
by the window. Below one dog's yapping at another,
plastering him with gurgling sounds. His mistress
is mumbling to herself as she pores over prices
in the jeweler's window display. I can see
her lips moving on the glass:
May a prayer help her. Dear God . . .
Just try to imagine a God
endowed with infinite talent. The second dog's
taking it lying down. Why doesn't he
run away? It's all experience,
and now he could easily make himself scarce. God's only
half human—for ever the same identical answers:
experience is, for Him, a term which has no meaning.
People are moving faster now, as though
some wind were propelling them, some invisible force.
They're all swimming past, all standing still,
turning their collars up in the teeth of the wind
that's taking their sentences along and turning them
into a simple universal answer.

THE PAINTER'S ALLOCUTION

I have, like so many before me, made sacrifices
to Beauty. My hand was the priest, an ascetic
locked into a cult of colors. It lived for dark surfaces—
down from bright-gray to bluish-black—and would not suffer
people and things. And in this way, canvas by canvas,
an ashen house got built—for Beauty, who never
herself showed up. Shall I make a new start?—
My work is done. The world is asleep
in the cup of my hand and twitches, blind-eyed,
when its dreams are oppressive. My picture is finished.
I won't paint again.

THE MUSEUM ATTENDANT'S ALLOCUTION

I've seen the world
in paintings. (And I've seen myself
in the salt-white eye of the hare
that pleads to live forever
as death sets in.)
I shared in every single death.

THE FOOL'S ALLOCUTION

Believe me, I can understand what the birds
are saying: the whistles, the trills of the nuthatch,
the thrushes' nervous chatter,
the wild refrain of the tawny owl
and the siskin's metallic patter
are not alien to me. When these creatures—
bashful at first and hesitant—
strike up their song of praise in the morning,
counterpointed by the magpies' raucous plaints
and the grating gossip of the crows,
when finches, warblers, buntings and larks
are at choir practice, I catch every word.
The doctors are at a loss.
They can't hear the linnet's command
(the one which shuts down day), can't fathom
the swifts' piercing cries
when they roll summer up to take
south with them. For those with ears, these notes
are signaling: fluting calls and scatterbrained flights
attract each other until a sentence comes into being,
a story—complete with a mating call and an admonition—
which takes to the air in feeble September,
some brownish chaff on the sky's
high canvas, easy to read in the wintertime.

THE TRANSLATOR'S ALLOCUTION
for Friedhelm Kemp

Over a hundred times I've
translated the moon, the poets'
friend, and haven't betrayed her.
I've made her melt into italics
or fattened her up with semibold type
when she was waning.
Have also, as best I could,
turned all those sighs—
since they're part of the language orbiting her—
into garrulous time.
Ahs! become her better than Ohs!—
statistically speaking, that is.
*All must be done anew, all
said anew* was my maxim.
I only got paid for one syllable:
moon.
Use only one term
for every concept, advises the head
of the Language Bank: it helps
the world to communicate.
Words are no one's property,
yet cost us dearly in terms of
hard cash. Demand for words rises
in proportion to GDP
so make economies where you can,
just leave it at:
moon.

THE ALLOCUTION OF THE DESPAIRING

There's no time left to make up for lost time:
the roads are too poor, the cart too small,
and all that's still with us is what fitted once
into a coat pocket. We sometimes wonder
what it could be: it feels cool and round
like the petrified head of some animal.
Where we now live, lost time would—in any case—
be out of place. In our new apartment
lives the Present. It's there at table
when we eat; It sweats Its way
though the night in our bed, dreaming
the better part of our dreams—
and when we go to work It crackles
softly between our files. When we finally
open our mouths to tell It what
we think, It speaks for us about Its goals.
When we're not watching, the Present
writes poems, using our pen,
to keep up on language. It got
the top prize from the Academy
for Its sonnet "Coldness Is the Future":
"History's a history of temperature."
Nature's aesthetically imperfect,
the poem claims, and grows impoverished, waxes,
mixes, at will. And only the breaking apart
of stones grants them their individuality.
Properly rhymed. And we, it concludes,
are the lumpy sand by the grave of identity.
Can we be blamed if we think so fondly
of lost time?

1995/2/1

Many thanks for your recent call.
I was so speechless because my sister
had only just died and, with her,
the gravity of the childhood we shared.
It makes you see how little is yours,
and what's left doesn't stretch to a story
with a beginning and end.
What's more, a winter storm was raging,
drowning out your friendly words.
The wind forced the trees to assume such postures
that even the birds lost all composure.
Relief was written all over their faces
when they could stand up straight again.
And, lastly, for days now, the heating's been seized
with Homeric sobs, as though some narrative were imprisoned
inside and were desperate to be released.
A singular dialect only spoken
within the confines of this house.
I'm still working, yes, and can't see myself
breaking off till the curtain.
A while back, I read that philosophers
would be content to merely hit on
one or two new questions—I'm dying
for answers though. The faintest echo
of a single feeble answer
that leaped into my face and stayed there
would be enough.

FEBRUARY '95

At the point where the rivers,
all foam, go crashing into each other,
changing their names,
there is—when the water level's high—
a tiny self-contained pool
that's not worth mentioning:
a child of the thaw.
A quiet resting place
for aquatic birds
that don't seem to know
which flood they
should take to
reach the sea.
For me, with my doubts,
there is a bridge—
a concrete leviathan
which, in a high arc,
is breaching nature.

AT NIGHT, BENEATH TREES

Trees, a loose series,
grouped as though afraid of space
on the downward slope.
One star, already bought from
the mighty skull of Night—
brought by the screech owl.
Words keep faith while things
flood into you;
none betrays you or itself.
Only at the end of this night
spent out under trees
does your mental fog rise
because no questions pester
the answer.

NOTE FOR THE FILES

At night I again heard
the screams of the birds,
and the grass listened in.
Armistice, loaded
with a live word,
an enduring one. For fifty years
we've been fed by Hitler;
it's time for the others
to eat, and we'll watch
their ugly convulsions,
a fork in each neck.
At night I again heard
the screams of the birds,
the winged epic poem
of Angst.

MEMORY OF CIORAN

He laughed his fill in the face of Creation.
Every broken stalk was a proof,
every dewdrop a tear,
every letter a bombshell.
Not to even mention Christ,
who loved him like a brother
that has to be sacrificed
to prove one's power.
A kick was the watermark
in his writing, slapstick gags
forever repeated: for years on end
he shed sleepless tears about Creation,
and now has died peacefully in his sleep.

EDUCATION

I'm not one of those
who desired his mother or
longed to kill an intrusive father.
Parental intercourse? Heaven knows,
it was other fantasies which drove me
out of the house. And the burst of light
the comet came with in the night sky
did not seem like an ejaculation.
The rainbow, too, which means so much,
did not join man and woman (or wife)
but heaven and earth.
Yet sometimes I ask myself
whether my ear knows what it's hearing,
my eye what it's seeing.
When I see Mary breast-feeding
her child, I fail to believe
that the body—the talked-to-pieces body—
of Christian culture has
given up its soul. And lastly:
that melancholy dog, my dog,
must not be some kind of subservient son!
Everyone has to come up with something
he or she thinks is true, overtly or covertly,
but there's only one thing which counts in the end:
the inscrutable world.

RUMOR, '95

A ghost is abroad
in Germany: it's said
to be small and to speak
in hurt, disabled words
like a foreign child.
And they say it's wearing
a coat, far too big
for its senile body.
And walking in boots,
laced up to the limit,
which tap in a shrill rhythm
on cranial sutures—
a rhythm that we're not meant to know.
Does not know its way around,
goes plucking the calendar
with a nimble finger.
Does not know its
name, and laughs
when it sees us—
sees how we are looking at it.
Is not from round here.

FAR FROM PERENNIAL VERSES

Far from perennial verses, unaware
of direction and factionless: oblivious,
they follow a path into the dark and suddenly
surface, transformed, in a clearing. They feel no craving
for burnished phrases, neglect to say
what people should do, and what they should not.
And when the Death of God's being mooted,
the Death of Man, they can't be heard.
Plato, Nietzsche, all those poets who fight
fire with fire—so sonority, higher forms, may emerge
from the febrile crepitation—despise
such far from perennial verses. But they still live on
in the lidbeats of the eye which keeps opening,
closing.

TO ZBIGNIEW HERBERT

Because a slight, slow-moving brook
often changes out of all recognition
in spring, in the weeks when the thaw sets in,
becoming a prepotent flood which ravishes
both banks while thrusting forcibly though,
there are many, tired of the present, who are now
staring at the dwindling supply of dreams
in the hope that there's something down at the bottom,
a different language underneath language,
enabling one to explain why we feel the urge
to explain (as though enough were not enough).
Not the routine we know as life,
the unfaithful head that's a wide-holed sieve
so we greet the sun each morning
with a fresh "Ah!," a fresh "Oh!"
Many of those who've had a first peep
into the brain conclude that the world is a hallucination;
at once they're lost in the Virtual
where trees are only look-alikes.
And on the border?
Stands a mirror the size of the world,
displaying a tree that isn't one:
what used, in our hand, to go by the name of reality
can't be distinguished any longer from the illusion
of that reality. Has the world changed
since the man from Media came—or just
our knowledge about the world, the knowledge
which makes it disappear as it goes
its repetitive way? Soon, dear Zbigniew,
we'll cover all this country's mirrors,
and turn all paintings to face the wall,
so the image they throw of us
won't deter the man who eventually
makes worlds which can't be imagined.

WRITERS' CONGRESS
Lahti / Finland

Once, surreptitiously, from my window—
in-ex-or-able brightness of the midsummer night—
I listened to the poets discoursing on beauty,
on its insulted truth, on the blotchy lawn
of the hotel. To the small-eyed Russian
who carried his shadow under his arm, as only
a Russian oppressed by the ill will of chalky small hours
can balance a shadow. When words reach us
sleepers, touch shore between two breaths
in morning's soft swell, that mood
of unity/endlessness surfaces,
out of which poems grow like gaunt grass
in crack-filled asphalt. To a sad Swede
who looked like the silent god of identity,
weary of playing with words. Just a breath still,
a syllable, one slight echo in a series of mirrors
which show no beginning, know no end.
To a Portuguese woman in flowing shawls
who spoke of the fluttering movements of the female hawk
on being first covered: that's how words conceive
our meaning, as a branch in spring
penetrated by earth's sap. And finally
to a poet from Poland, with eyes for truth only
(for truth, that's not found in sentences): a man
with dark eyes, who'd got lost in the maze of his melancholy.
To throw light on the predicament of poetry,
he showed the others a coin: no sign
of head or tail on that well-worn disk.
A requiem for the empty space between
spirit and nature underneath a blue-gray sky.
For my part, I (with my head out of sight behind the curtain)
had one or two things on the tip of my tongue regarding the claim
to truth of poetic discourse, but I kept my mouth shut,
and warmed the nascent screams in my mouth
which formed one part of the truth, whose history
is known as sanguinary error. A powerless part—
ransacked, profaned, unable to sew what's been rent
back together. But I couldn't speak, and only saw
my own face in the window's mirror, vague
as molten pitch. And later—it was long

past midnight—a sleep-starved French poet
joined the others. He'd been collecting
pebbles down by the lake in the bright night,
hounded by the rasping cries of seagulls.
He showed them his trouvailles: we're outside literature
when we talk about it, he said (every word
was audible); we just replicate it, fail
to touch its heart—its hard, indestructible core.
Let us be guests, uninvited but welcome,
fortuitous guests who take a seat
and vanish again without being missed.
The Pole said nothing. The Russian first released his shadow
then skipped after it. The Portuguese woman, wrapped up like a mummy,
was probably thinking of the words which celebrate
the body's beauty, unimpressed by death. The Swede
departed smiling like someone who knows
the frailty of what he is doing. I remained standing
behind the window and watched the wind,
which found peace in the bright green of the birch trees.

THE CEMETERY

Right by the entrance, adjoining the compost heap
where gladioli exhale their stuffy sweetish redness,
a poet I knew well lies buried. He'd brought
a couple of words back from the war
(concealed in a show), and these he massaged
till a book took shape: sixty-four pages,
along with an entry—dropped after his death—in the queen
of encyclopedias. His elegiac tone was lauded,
his images, his provenance from Oskar Loerke
(whom he never met). We owe him
spurious rhymes, for a spurious life too.
("A herald" was what Benn called him, but the letter's
been lost, so there is no culprit behind
the crime). Though never monied, he had his muses
who washed his dishes and sent off his poems
while he sprawled, washed-out and sad, on the sofa.
He sensed the stony look that was fixing him
from the future, bleaching his words.
One row behind there's a colleague who, way back in the sixties,
made poetry concrete: God's a word too,
a field day for the atheists.
Long word-chains scattered across the page,
and the last link, with nowhere to go:
a tidbit for academics, who likened
his poems to sand, to desert, for whatever reason.
He was, when you met him, always returning from a congress
or traveling to a symposium in somewhere like Celle,
strictly second-class, weighed down by lexica
he'd be digging over with sharp fingers, searching
for singular treasures—"oblatio" for "burnt offering,"
you don't understand that you must understand.
He drank himself to death. His name, in lower-case letters,
has lost some characters already:
that would no doubt have pleased him. (An anthology
came out in São Paulo recently, in which he's extolled
as a permanent revolutionary).
His wife, a more conventional talent, wrote
poems too. In one she compared a person's slowness
with the blinking of an owl. My God,
what vitriol oozed from the critics;
the mildest rebuke was plagiarism.

But whom do words belong to? She's probably
still alive and is washing the blood, with gouty fingers,
from the marble.—Next to the wall that abuts on the road,
awash in the uproar he so often sang of, lies the grave
of the city's sole political poet.
He was a real star, got learned by heart—
each poem he wrote was a tender punch, brief,
dry and telling: the world reveals its set of brown teeth.
He was my neighbor for two years, then he moved to the country
or rather let himself be moved by a woman who nowadays
forges his signature in order to pay the rent.
I couldn't find a grave. And the gardener shook
his head. "A poet? Here? I've no idea
if poets are buried round here, the gravestones
don't tell you, you know." They say he hanged himself.
"Accident" said his family, which could afford
to buy up and stamp out his books of poems.
I was in Rome with him in the eighties:
he fashioned long poems on emperors, popes
and cats in a language so outlandish,
so scintillating, that no one could grasp them. Now
there are some who pride themselves on having always
seen his talent: they praise his high style,
encompassing hatred, beauty and grief in the classical manner,
purifying your vision. I can still hear him laughing,
talking of critics who think that there's progress in poesy,
apart from perceiving the flight of birds that was making its way
from the station toward the Colosseum, where he lived.
Bird flight, script that erases itself . . . No sign of his
grave. And what did that leave? He'd given me
a poem, a pretext of death, dressed in rhyme,
written in the dark, *in the light from the eyes of a cat*—
it occurred to me then. Outside the cemetery
stood a telephone booth, shining bright; I went inside,
removed the receiver from its cradle and slowly
talked my heart out.

LAST DAY OF THE YEAR

As though the sky were bent on indemnifying the earth,
the rain today has washed all paintings out of frames
which now circumscribe bright patches on the streaky walls.
The world that will come! Only memories keep
their muddy color. The year clogs up in its final hours.
Let nobody say there's plenty of space between cup and lip
when only a handsbreadth separates progress
from tripping in circles;
the fact is (and this is not a lesson we needed to learn)
that every day a new year begins: the year of war.
It's not an allegory either, like the lounging angel
clamped in a gas mask in smiling galaxies. Now,
the trump which blacks out one-third of the sun can be heard,
one-third of the moon, one-third of the stars
without anybody noticing, and—as to the rest—
it implodes like the green dot on TV when the news is over,
the year's last news. And Grace, who loves her enemies too,
has got the date wrong, her deceptive glibness has stut-
tered her into the new year, with the conqueror
reconquered long since: dragged in chains, for all to see,
across the ocher marketplace of images,
trailing his blood. On the eyes of this dead man
landscapes are growing, an eminent ruin, the rhyming whispering
of the palm trees, a well without words, shaded-in, crosshatched,
captured by our premier painter, who's shyly hiding
behind his camera. Ça va mal, très mal, quoth the demiurge—
he who once again spells what's illegible, makes a fair copy:
obituaries for the eye only. Another hour. It's time for our
foes to show up. Life's disappeared
from the earth and is only now to be found in the depths of the ocean.
Was it Kant who saw us surviving on Jupiter?
At any rate, Destiny's off the agenda, we're too deep
in debt, and the drifting pack ice is spreading,
spreading farther and farther. Maybe, who knows, this special
moment was also born of a sign from above—
this second in which we finally pitch down
into silence. I watch the rain, the hedge the wind is maltreating;
the night which, heavy-tongued,
is working its salvage
so that the new year
can bring its old self.

Richard Dove

from *Shortly Before the Storm*
2003

WHERE I WAS BORN

1

My grandfather could tell more than
a hundred birds by their song, not counting
the dialects spoken in the hedgerows,
dark schools behind the yard,
where the whinchats were on duty.
My grandfather was an expert on potatoes.
He dug them out with his hands, split them
with his thumbs that turned white
and told me to lick at the break.
Floury, good for pigs and people.
Even after the expropriation he wanted, more than
anything, to believe in God, that's why I was sent
to dig up potatoes from the field that used to be his.
Like on Dutch paintings, heavy clouds
moved across the Saxon sky,
coming from Russia and Poland
heading West, their load growing lighter,
finer, more sheer, until in France
they'd be sold as silk. In the West, he would say,
things are changing, we are being changed.
Some of his friends from the village went missing.
They were made to load clouds in Russia.

2

My grandmother used irons
to curl her thinning hair. Your hair
must look its best when you meet your maker.
He would come mostly at night, when I
was supposed to be asleep, and sit on the
edge of the bed chatting with her in Saxon.
The pair of them whispering as if they had secrets.
Sometimes they were on friendly terms,
and then she would quarrel with him as she did
with grandfather, when he placed his glass eye
next to his plate on the table. When you put it in
back to front, you can look inside,
into your head, where your thoughts reside,
he would say, and stuff his pipe with home-grown
that hung on the wall by the table, messy leaves,
on a thread. The sleeves of grandfather's

outdoor jacket were scarred with burn holes.
Just like your lungs, grandmother said,
both of them brown. And so time passed.
In the evenings it was potatoes with sauce or without.
When it was time for slaughter up at the farm,
belly of pork appeared on my plate,
but I wasn't to ask how we'd come by it.
Pork belly can fly, say no more.
I imagined God as a person,
who took everything in his stride.

    3

My grandfather no longer bothered to read. All the books
are in my head, he'd say, but jumbled up.
Instead, he liked to tell stories, his favorites about the King,
who was said to have shown an interest in him.
During the hunt it was his job to drive
a hare in front of the guns, but grandfather
had hidden the creature under his jacket.
Even today I can hear the hare's heart beating,
he'd cry and touch the spot where his watch
hung. Hares have bad hearts,
not something you could count on. Nor the state
either. When grandmother wasn't with us
we'd listen to the radio, voices like knives,
that made the plume of his pipe smoke quiver.
Bloody swine, my grandfather said, who never otherwise
swore. Music was at home in the vicinity of Beromünster,
let's go there one day, he would say,
and hear Bach and Tchaikovsky. Then fell asleep,
the lid over his glass eye never quite closed.

    4

When I returned to my village not so long ago,
it all came back to me, just jumbled up:
ersatz honey, and the thick black syrup that dripped
through the holes in the bread, the spitting fires
over Meuselwitz, the Cyrillic machine guns in the quarry
near Keyna, the coal dust, warm beer, a fearful God,
the squawking alarm cry of the hoopoe,
the throbbing threads on the back of grandfather's hands,

the blue carpet under the plum trees,
the dog-eared pages of the Bible, the pious poverty,
the joy. The dead joined in too, arriving from far away
in old-fashioned clothes, the women with hairnets,
the men with their uniforms turned inside out,
and bullet holes in their sunken breast.
And in the midst of it all my grandfather, one eye
on the world, the other turned inwards, before him
a plate of potatoes, floury and yellow with butter,
good for pigs and people and me.

5
I am all that, the man with the heart of a hare.
Not more, and if anything less.

SHADOW AND LIGHT

I knew someone once, who knew of nothing
darker than light, and that he studied
throughout his life with his shortsighted eyes.
He buried himself in the deepest shadow
of the Talmud and beavered like a humble
workman at the bearded writings of Gnosis,
until he too resembled one of the letters
that does not know God.
He taught me the origin of the light in
Vermeer's paintings, a light that is always unique.
His brief, clever essays concerning the alcove,
the corner, and the veil were read by the moths
that fly up out of learned tomes,
his fragmentary novel is unparalleled.
Every day we would visit the well,
where, the story goes, the maid had fallen
as she stared up at the stars, and nothing
unsettled him more than the ants
that kept on turning the globe.
When the candle, by which he'd written
his work, went out, he gave himself over
at last, to the light, in which he did not believe.

MOVING OUT

Now the rooms are empty, suitcases
stand in the hall next to stubborn crates,
where books fight with newspapers.
An unequal struggle: paper against paper,
the playing out of an old tragedy.

How the emptiness reeks! A housefly
flies in circles taking photographs,
an angel with a black flag,
besotted with humming liturgy.
On the window sill a coin,
the old currency, that buys anything.

No chair, no bed here asking for forbearance,
even memory has crumbled away
like a termite. Did someone once live here?
Soon evening will move in
erase the imprint of the pictures
that we took down,
and will never hang up again.

TWO RED FISH AND ONE BLACK

The fisherman returns, in his net
two red fish and one black,
the night's catch: a present for me.
Now he darns a thousand silvery
bodies into his torn net. I'm reading.
"By image," I read, "we mean anything
that serves as a vehicle
to give access to something else."
The river bank disappears, the dream.
With his gnarled fingers he tears
open the heavens, our true home,
and shows me the last of the sorry
utopias.

NIGHT STOP

We stopped en route. Above
the table hung a sticky fly-trap
with its thousand dead stories.
The waiter was speechless, not
a bite to eat. One of us
said: as for us, we're still miles
away from life. We set the bottle
spinning, it pointed at me.
In the distance you could hear
the steady drone of the motorway,
coming ever closer.
If I'm not mistaken, we may not
have made it out of there unhurt.

ARRIVAL

The town is almost deserted.
The petrol stations in the center
dispense only hatred,
take an unknown currency.
Grass and stinging nettles
lay siege to the pumps,
the counters practice a language
no one here understands.
The attendant wants to teach
a lesson in silence.
He stares in concentration
at the sky, as if he were trying
to read something there.
Our shadows are short
under the noonday sun.

BRIDGE

A narrow bridge only connects
darkness with darkness. And a light that
dissolves the world into tiny points
which we struggle to connect
to make a picture—as if we had
the right to a picture in a solid frame.
And from the north, blown in over the jetty,
unintelligible words, childhood words,
dipped in honey and held up into the wind;
they reach us, here, upon the bridge
that connects darkness with darkness.
Below, the water wears away the sharp edges
from the pebbles, so they are carried further
and lose themselves in the sea.
How tiny the bridge that connects
your eyes—it's like a cry
at a wordless fear, no more.

THE ENGLISH GARDEN, MUNICH

A frown darts across
the pensive land,
summer departs
in a policeman's uniform.
Insects nettle words
into religious chatter,
sheep stand about
as though mislaid,
and night falls
like a buzzard from the sky.
A group of stragglers
hang back, they don't know
what they have in their midst,
inviting death into the grass.

VISIT TO THE GRAVEYARD

A grave has been opened, the workmen
stand with both legs in the pit, looking
up at me from down below. The hidden things
are slowly unearthed, brought to light
in red hands. Clumps of soil, snails,
wood and a handful of bones, nothing
to frighten us. Had I hoped for more?
As a child I always wanted to know
what it is that disappears with the dead,
never to return, the sacred things of life.
I carry on, my shadow of its own accord
searching out other bodies,
balanced, like a sleepwalker,
on the green ridge between the graves.

SUMMER'S END

The epistles to the light become
longer again, stitched into giddy
leaves; stories follow the sun,
light and talkative,
the ambiguous feast has blown away.
The world of possibilities grows
with the shadows. Just one person says:
let everything stay as it was.
The wind picks at our clothes
like a thief and the water
has no time now for discretion.

WOMAN READING

When I think of you I see
a woman reading in shadow.
She keeps a language under her tongue
that doesn't avoid the dark.
She reads so softly I can hear her:
"They smiled at me like dead men smile
when they see we believe
they are no longer alive."
The letters rise up before her eyes
and desert the book she is reading,
the very moment I think of you.

THE CROSS

In old churches in the south
I sometimes cross myself
to ease my conversation with
the sacred. It works. Then I chat
awhile with the saltpeter angels
who live in damp corners,
in a mixture of humility
and orthodoxy. In Barcelona
cathedral, Santa Milena stepped
out of her dust-covered fresco,
a girl, to sit with me
on the cold marble steps of the altar.
We had to whisper. Around us
old ladies clutched their string bags
instead of rosaries. It smelled
of mint, of incense and oranges.
Milena pointed to a traveler,
in a gloomy painting staring at a lightning
bolt, a viper writhing through the sky.
That will be you, she said, that is the path
you must follow, but don't be afraid,
I will wait for you here.

LAST THINGS

My house has six doors,
all built of solid wood.
The first bargained too long
with the architect over where
it should stand and was closed.
The second is allergic to light
and won't open during the day.
The third stands ajar only in dreams
to reveal an ancient bearded angel
going about his duty.
The fourth leads to an ideal world
and is no longer used.
The fifth is seeking its form
by the old measure of the possible.
The sixth is invisible.
For years now I've felt my way
round the walls, trying to find it.
I have no doubt that it exists.
Of course it would be possible
to give the house another door,
as my friends all advise me to do.
But I'd rather tear the house down
and seek entrance in the rubble.

TOO LATE

It is already past midnight,
the hands of the clock catch
their breath. A snail sets off
and takes away all the ashen words
until the sheet of paper is white again,
an atlas of emptiness.
I have little time.
Like the water that seeps
from stone in spring, the dawn
comes trickling in.
Wide awake, I go to sleep.

REST

The lake is choked with weed and a stillness
nests among the reeds, as if the lesson
had been well learned: not another word
about the time that is lost. Only the rushes
nod like Jews at prayer, a mournful utopia
of motion. The water withdraws,
the sky hangs heavy and low
over the fields and a pale moon
braves the ashen cloud.
A war rages in town, you see
how the blaze competes with the darkness.
But that's not even the start.

HOW WAS IT?

We sat too long at table, as always
when it's a matter of art and life.
Each had something to say,
each held something back.

Someone stood up. Stood with both feet
between earth and heaven, wordless
and helpless, as if to prove
his own frailty.

Above us—we sat in the garden—
the birds formed a trembling ladder
that, light and fluent,
vanished into the clouds.

REVIEW

In light of how things are panning out
it is time to make plans
for this year and the year before.
There's a book to be read,
the compassion quota to be lowered.
We don't want to die by mistake,
we say, shaking our heads.
Our fears are unfounded,
for certain, the others say.
What is certain? Alone in the
dark we ransack old dictionaries
for the exact meaning of happiness.

AT NIGHT

As sleep drags itself groaning
from room to room
the waking hours whisper
with a foreign moon.
Now is the time for a boat
to set sail in the gray-washed sky
far away from any human warmth.

JUST SHORTLY BEFORE THE STORM

A gentle rain and the cedar,
embroidered into evening with a thousand
stitches plus one, loses its calm.
Even the stones move out
in search of a shore. Only the
rooks with their naked, white faces
resolve to stay back. They tug
the cover shrouding the world
as though there were something to show.
All that's still visible recalls
the invisible that will stay
invisible for good, when the storm
breaks.

REALITY SHOW

for Peter von Matt

Wolves live in the garden now.
How cute, we say, as we watch
them lick their bloody paws.
Their stench spreads like gas.

One has a duck in its claws,
another two blackbirds. Bad luck.
We turn to nature for counsel,
but the sun keeps itself to itself

and the rain has moved into town.
Hungry creatures. Their eyes shining
like ink and blood. At night they lie
under the apple tree noisily

grinding their teeth.

TO WHOM IT MAY CONCERN

Even when we know we shouldn't,
we are fond of looking back: the streets
are narrower, the houses smaller,
the big issues disappear before our eyes.
With a world behind us the living
is easier, war is a game,
even blood is simply
a stain of red on the screen.
We admire the vivid blue
over the distant shore. Being pious
alas, was never for us, the lore
of flowers, fields, the hedgerows,
of no importance now.
The letters that made off with our
misery betray a foolish need for clarity.
Look, the column of ants,
voracious and curious, nothing can
stand in their way.

PASSAGE

The snow began to smoke,
a blue-tinged veil lay over the white.
We were getting nowhere,
the wheels whined and went into a spin.
One of us wrote in his diary:
nothing for miles but hesitant grief.
Some tried their luck on foot,
their shadows passing with ease
along the path of the moon, over the mountain.

APPLICATION

I've got nothing to hide:
my fatigue is congenital,
my eyes an open sore,
my c.v. went missing
between previous jobs.
My ego calls my habit
of dissolving the triumph
of misery over pain.
The only secret I have
is as tame as an old mutt,
it wouldn't hurt a fly
and stays out of sight.
I'm still good for twenty years,
after that let's play it by ear.
It's an enduring mystery
that people can live together
without asking forgiveness
for this intolerable condition.

POETICS, SEPTEMBER 1998
for Wulf Segbrecht

1

Goethe's birthday behind us and exchange rates
in freefall. The dollar is now the unofficial currency.
The pain threshold is with the snowline at 1300 meters,
and down on the flatland we're already under water.
Veba, Fontane, Rheinstahl, everything's falling, Novalis
is no longer quoted. And what do they make of Celan?
They say the classical repertoire is already on the skids,
Karajan, Celibidache, the great violin virtuosos, names
no one knows any more. And yet good Dr. Kohl wants
to help take the Ring in Bayreuth into the next
century. Only the car industry is booming big time,
since it's been manufacturing escape cars that collapse
on arrival. Nothing but rain. Even in parliament
the smell of wet wool. In cellars in Bonn they want
to grow mushrooms, or that's what is rumored
in the circles that are generally in the know for
the market is our destiny. Our mandala.
Forced laborers are now being paid with delay,
but could they please line up in an orderly fashion.

2

It's becoming ever easier to imagine a world
without people. All that can be crammed in your skull,
into the white slats to right and left,
would remain: the leftovers on the plate, the sunbeam.
Through the keyhole, the small dark name
for love. The bronze-yellow moss on the pantheon,
a few verses begged from memory.
You're woken up by the icy cold and discover
that death is sleeping next to you, eyes open.
You could leave all the hidden values blank
because no one is moved by them any more.
You would always be knocking at doors, with people
living behind them, sometimes you'd hear the TV
inside, its white noise. This, for example, is where
the enemy lived. Now that even he's left you,
there are only victories. Everywhere weeds, luxuriant growth

in overgrown gardens. Long lazy strolls
in the company of snails, blackbirds and hares.
How polite the animals are! How engaging! They've read
Nietzsche and Plato and Kant. And they ask you
quite seriously, where on earth everyone is?
And then you come to the sea.
From far away you see the empty ships,
bowing to one another, the gray coast
under a gray sky. An old pair of sandals,
now home to crabs, a plastic bottle, nothing else
to be found. You would hunker down there
and write a poem in the sand, like so many
you've written before, but far enough from the water,
your contribution to immortality.

     3
An angel sits in the garden and cries,
that misfortune and misfortune will not rhyme

ON DREAMS

My grandfather, a down-to-earth farmer
with hands dry as sandpaper,
claimed he would dream only
other people's dreams.
Those were miserable times, the war
had left its heavy artillery scattered
round the farm, and many had forgotten
what they had forgotten.
Almost anything could be done without:
questions, coffee and warmth, for sure.
Desires too, so as not to disturb
the peace. But that anyone,
in all seriousness, should claim
that he could do without his own dreams,
was laying it on thick, even in our neck of the woods.

UNEXPECTED ENCOUNTER

We knew each other at a time
when the brightness was still our own.
In those days we wrote dark poems
about the invasion of light
that we learned off by heart.
And every evening we made
an outing to the empty terrain
of philosophy, right outside our door.
We bumped into each other at the post office.
He wanted to get shot of a letter
that he'd written at the time,
I was looking for his phone number.
The queue swallowed us up
and tore us apart with a woman and child
who wanted to hand themselves in.
An unusually hot summer
stripped the memory from our bodies.
The rest would fit on a postcard.

ON BEAUTY

for Charles Simic

A man sat by the carpark
on an upturned bucket
grilling me fiercely
on the nature of beauty.
The sun shone solemnly
into his weary face.
Something that does not
fit with anything else, I wanted
to say, but kept my mouth shut
and slipped a coin in his hand
that wouldn't let go.
We drank beer out of cans.
Above us in the linden tree
the raucous croaking of crows
that will not die away
in spite of the serious questions.

WHAT THE AGGRIEVED MAN SAYS

I am aggrieved.
All attempts to cheer me up
have been in vain.
People keep asking
why don't you laugh.
What about, I reply,
I don't want to haggle
with hope.
Because I'm sleepless,
I go walking at night.
I hear animals breathing,
the shadows whisper to me.
One time I found … but no,
let's not go into that.

MAX SEBALD IS DEAD

A writer has died
in the midst of his text.
To comfort us
the others must be silent,
though not forever,
but right now.

EPITAPH FOR A POET

Before our eyes he rose up
from his deathbed to add a
final comma, then he could sleep.
Today his work is forgotten.

WHAT THE HISTORIAN SAYS

Everything I could lay my hands on
I've dragged from the past into the present.
I've read files, studied documents,
parlayed with barbarians
and their enemies, our friends.
My pencil has worn to a stub,
the eraser's used up, the inkwell
is dry. I wanted to find out why we are
how we are.
When my work was complete
it was like a darkened mirror.
I even stood my ground when I
looked round and caught sight of myself,
a failure without end.

THE ELEVENTH COMMANDMENT

Thou shalt
not die,
please.

Karen Leeder

74

from *Under an Open Sky*
2007

from *MEDITATIONS UNDER AN OPEN SKY*

*

The light is ready at last
to open itself to the dark,
as a higher mechanics demands.
From the woods I hear
the deer's dry coughing,
in the copper dusk
the last attachments dissolve.
There are no rules
for you to hold onto,
that is the message
from time as it races by.
Above me in a childlike sky,
a helicopter hovers,
army or archaeology, not important now.
Once people were settlers here,
sometimes even now they
step out of the woods in the darkness
and rattle their old bones.
The ground has stored the heat.
Memory skips past
so its feet do not burn.

*

Just a moment ago we stood
laughing under the pine candelabras
admiring the silvery frost
that coated the branches, when the fog
came in all at once. The sky grew ever more
incomplete, the pictures
melted before our eyes.
The air was like smoke, impenetrable
and soft. We stood rooted to the spot
and waited for judgment.

*

A hundred times the oriole rehearses
the misfortune of mastery.
Then in a flash he curves away,
a yellow gash in the universe
that will never heal.

*

For days now great black birds
have occupied the land.
Unmoved, they take the words
out of our mouths.
What was it we wanted to say?
Who we wanted to be
before blood and thunder
became our neighbors,
one to the left, one right.
Now time slips away from us
without a word. The birds, unmoved,
talk themselves into their
world of black.

*

In the pond the motionless newts,
circled by water spiders
that take the place of clocks. A drowned
mouse. Wasps building
Jacob's ladder, so their souls
can ascend. A blessing,
they say, cannot be revoked.
But what gives us the right
to betray almost everything
so we can save ourselves. How I long
for the night, the good night of thinking,
when history goes to sleep.

NATURE PIECE

A buzzard hovers on the horizon.
It sees the hare zigzag across the meadow,
Time takes to its heels.
A mouse crouched in perennial weeds.
It sees every ant, the movable sum
of sleeplessness. It sees smaller birds,
whose cries could waken the dead.
And sees us, fine upright creatures,
to whom the truth means everything.
Sees how we stand open-mouthed.
Nothing more to be said.

*

We will never learn,
that was what they concluded at a congress
on the other side of the world.
No one knew whether to be sad,
as everyone had half known anyway.
Swallows, thin as compass needles,
hung for days in the air.
Everything went wrong, almost everything.
We can do nothing to stop the river
taking the light downstream,
and at night the insects stick to our eyes
and mouths as we stand in the dark at a loss,
at the far side of sleeplessness.
Thank God we only have a dim idea
of what we are, that would be the end.

*

We arrived upright
a gaggle of admirers
seeking imperfection, we let snow
color our imaginings
blackberries our pain.
We got stuck in
until exhaustion polished
our faces, breathed in, breathed out
and had to leave again.

SUMMER

We should be happy. Above us the maple
waving with a thousand hands, and above that
a shrouded sky, content with all the roles
and capable of being wrong.
Crickets saw at the shadow. And midges
weave the death mask of summer.
A jay doles out orders with a laugh:
Don't accept it! It takes years
before the message can be heard: too much
is ending and too little begins.

VISITING POET

He pitches up out of the blue as always
and tells us the story of the river
that flows towards his name,
but never reaches it.

I am that river, the poet says,
as if we hadn't guessed.
Keep an eye, or he'll pocket the lot,
his appetite for things is insatiable.

What evokes grandeur or deserves
respect, he finds disconcerting, then
babbles on about water fleas and reeds.

He flows through our house for three days
and for three days we look at one another,
without knowing who we are.

TELL THE SPARROW HAWKS

for Wolfgang Bächler

Tell the sparrow hawks
they should stop the clock
when I die,
and the falcon, my friend,
should split the dial
before lightning strikes.
There is a hidden sentence
in every friendship
that is never spoken,
never.
So things stood
between us.

A FRIEND

He wanted to live in a hotel, by the sea,
and breakfast each day with other guests
who'd spread their dreams on toast for him
while he ate his soft-boiled egg in silence.
No books, no post, no certainties,
and when the maid had left
the room: he'd write a page
pop it straight into an envelope, return
address, as usual, not the hotel.

He died in town, in an old people's home,
ears stopped against beautiful words.
The notebooks and scribblings
we found in his effects
tell of his friendship with swallows
and the daily visits of death.
One entire page devoted to thrift,
Armeria vulgaris, bereft of beauty,
not even pleasant as tea.

80

WALK

with Richard Pietraß

Up on top: no view,
the world has all died out.
Once people spoke of saints,
but what might they look like today?
Was the way up here perhaps
just a descent after all?
Back to the rivers.
Why should the water care?
It runs ahead of misfortune
into the afternoons, the evening.
What we no longer use
is taken up by the poplar,
patient tree, that never asks
what we need.
Let he who believes what he says
when he's lying, step forward
then darkness can fall.

AS POEMS WERE ONCE MEANT TO ILLUMINATE THE WORLD

As poems were once meant to illuminate the world
that did not exist, the pathway, sheltered by broom,
the silvery thistle, the rising and falling tides
the shuttered sky, torn open by the white
birds; just as later poems were meant to record
the bright strip of light under the door,
the stilled curve of the script, the heart,
shriveled by the advocacy of furious words;
just as poems, not so long ago, were meant
to give voice to what we couldn't own, the darkening,
the uninhabitable night, as the precondition of light,
chance as the law of probabilities;
now they must speak to themselves
in a language not their own,
in which we cannot forget ourselves.

WE'D AGREED TO MEET, THAT

We'd agreed to meet, that
night, between the villages,
under a waning moon.
She wanted to take her horse,
I was schlepping the suitcase.
I weighed each and every word.
They had to be light but not vague,
certain, but not too heavy.
The word love I learned by heart
so as not to have to use it.
On the ridge of cypresses
that stood like wicks in the earth,
we passed one another in silence.

BROUGHT UP A CHRISTIAN, MY GRANDFATHER

Brought up a Christian, my grandfather
loved the gentle stars.
Comets that tore open
the fine fabric of the heavens,
he loathed with all his heart.
Troublemakers, idiots, he'd grumble,
dug in behind his field glasses.
Grandmother, who stood by him,
had to listen out 'til break of dawn
for comets hurtling through
the universe, until the sun urged her
to bed.

THAT'S THE LAST PICTURE

That's the last picture
of my father and me.
We'd gone to the coast,
found a wicker chair and
sat for hours looking out across the sea.
My father spoke in a way
he'd never done before. It was good
listening to him. Painful too.
What had he wanted to tell me?
Not the slightest. But I knew
it was vital for both of us.
Later he'd written something
in the sand by the edge of the water,
he guessed that the waves
would erase the text straight away.

THE APPLE TREE

is felled, twelve apples still
hang in the branches.
A crow keeps death
from my life, my door.
The heavy steps of thought
in the grass.
As for me: I must hold my tongue.
The things left unspoken
wilt slowly in the shadows.

HOTEL FUTURE

Welcome, Sir! Are you traveling
in order to forget your worries
or do you take them with you when
you go? The porter has the kind of face
that care has turned its back on.

I know all the rooms by heart.
The Iliad is whispered in the pipes,
only the dying cry out with the heat.
One thing still to be done:
saving what is already lost.

Me, I'm on the uppermost floor
with the doves. Outside the
window a feverish sky buds.
Time has gone inland
to the stones that never sleep.

THE EMPTY HOUSE

The empty house stands like a vestry
before the mute organ of elms.
A school where one can learn how
poverty comes into being. A screech owl
sets the tone. War goes in and out,
without batting an eyelid. It smells
of beeswax and fresh cinnamon.
The shadows outstay their welcome.
In the distance the blustering laughter
of the sea. And always when I try to sleep
the choir strikes up its rehearsal.

SEPTEMBER SONG

Crows drop from the skies, like
they've been fed with lead.
We start to take superstitious
detours to come by bread and wine.
Soon we look like people
who never want to be found,
our faces growing darker
as though drawn in thick
chalk on a shady wall.
Books are losing their readers,
the letters take flight one by one,
thick gobs of glue on the ground.
Shall we turn round?
Strike for home, past the sour-faced crows,
and then just keep on going?

WHY DO YOU KEEP CHICKENS

"Why do you keep chickens
on the roof?" I asked
grandfather.
"If they lived down there,"
was his answer,
"they would have to eat
stones, up here they eat light."

WHAT FLOWS

In this part of the land there is too little water.
Grandmother placed a jug of corn poppies
on the shabby round table.
The yellow and red petals, already tired
from the journey, up two long flights,
in a tight fist and short of breath.
There was no running water,
it was my job to fetch it in pitchers,
without spilling a drop,
three pitchers for washing the body,
one for soup, one for dishes.
And one glass of water for their teeth,
that curious, bickering couple
that ended up together every evening in a glass.
The storms came from the East. Why from the East?
The back and forth of thunder and lightning,
windows open, in the garden
that just had been grandfather's domain;
then the downpour that filled the urns to overflowing.
And much later, before bed time,
the tears. The boy who wouldn't speak,
but stared at the petals,
that described a flaming circle round the vase.
In this part of the land there's too little water!
Hydraulics was the name of the art that I was to learn,
not medicine or social science.
And couldn't even find the words to give the vaguest
outline of the water, the way it was.

VILLAGE CINEMA

The garden gate was flung open:
birds flew up, giddy swallows
and robins in full fig.
Village cinema, we paid with apples
and our scabby knees. Then the other
guy entered the scene, the one we
weren't, the one with the ladder
who disappeared into the earth, hours
later you'd still hear him coughing.
He's probably lost his way and will
come back up where no one understands him.
His picture hung on cherry trees
and poplars until the ants carried
it away, bit by bit, like an exquisite
fresco, and left it unrecognizable.
Only the resilient nails remained
hammered in the bleeding wood.
That evening, when the light was folded,
corner to corner, someone came knocking
at the front door, with a shady
past and muddy shoes.
He brought rumors with him, hidden
under his tongue, and offered them up
in exchange for bread. Grandmother said
he'd once been a poet, one of those who load
flowers with words till their necks break.
After '49 the cinema was closed.

TV

The wind was cursing, and in my dreams
there were only the fallen and the dead.
A car scoured the corpse of the city
then turned back into the silence.
We learned the few words
one uses to listen.
Now the city burns and the flames
flutter like a child's hands.
A landing stage full of sparrows
shows the way to the future, a ship
sails past, it is loaded with lambs
who once dreamed of being wolves.

MEMORY

Age-old houses in rows
along inquisitive roads.
In the village someone said
that feelings were idle chat.
Pay no mind!
my grandfather said,
winter will soon be here.
We went fishing
before the frost. Just let
them talk, he would say,
with a long stare, in which
feelings scarcely troubled the surface.

COMET

A comet comes into view again—
bright (like a long-lost word)
rushing towards us.
It has nothing to fear.
The wind idly grooms the grass.
And we are out to find cities
where we'd prefer not to die.

IN THE SWISS ALPS

Like an old friend the fog came
towards us, a mute, formless matter,
that shaped us after its own desires.
We had no time to hunt for a path,
trees passed us by, without haste,
as though on tip-toe, root systems
slung round their whispering crowns
and stones, freshly plucked from the
earth, showed off their bearded riches.
Implacable fog, extolling the beauty
of what we can't see, the chortling stream
and the timid, twittering birds.
Staring blindly, shy and forlorn,
no idea which way to turn, we saw only
our hands in front of our eyes in the fog.

A LONG NIGHT

The night shows no sign of ending,
and the clamor of birds that once
brought light to our room, a gift,
is nowhere in sight. Not so far away
darkness is milled from future and time,
a steady humming without content or form.
The miller sleeps. His ancient beard
crawling with stories, that crackle
like fire, stories of war that revolve
in your head. Too much history
woke us up, and now we sit at table
and shiver, wait for a blitz to save us,
make us visible again. Can you hear the world?
someone asks, but who, cannot be seen.

THE HOUSE WAS TOO COLD

The house was too cold,
my paper-thin sleep
couldn't warm up the roof tiles.
I'd rowed across the lake
with the last of the birds,
but silence had put them to flight.

NOTHING HAS HAPPENED

Nothing has happened
that could be written down.
Just sometimes the world
is so big that words
got lost in it.
That's when I go to the lake
to watch the ducks.
When the little ripples
they make in the water
reach the bank, I stretch out
in the tall grass and am
nowhere to be found.

DELPHIC ORACLE

The cricket, queen of false witness,
can't grasp a word of the sermons
it preaches for hours.
And unruly gnats rejoice in the fact
that God came into the world too late.
I don't know in whose name
I speak, nor at whose behest,
says the Delphic Oracle.
In its pale moth-eaten robe,
the future grows out of the stones
and doesn't even spare us a glance.
All the words have been written,
but they've never been spoken out loud.

THE DICTATOR'S LAST SPEECH

One knows too little about oneself.
Today, for example, I'm no longer sure
of myself and hereby proclaim
that all portraits of me
should be turned to the wall
until this order is revoked.

17 June 1996

Since the dictator died shortly afterwards without ever having encountered himself face to face,
the portraits in all official institutions have remained back to front to this very day.

Karen Leeder

from *Fair Copy*
2010

FLEABANE

Sometimes I think of the fleabane
that grew, I recall, in my youth,
at those spots where boundary stones
had been moved for private purposes.

Moved sometimes at pain of death.

Fleabane, not an especially lovely plant,
it is scarcely known today.
Yet it's still there! When I tried, not long ago,
to change my life a little, I saw it blooming.

ON THE LAKE

1

Time drifts past us,
heedless,
towards the waves that
meet again behind the boat,
without a backwards glance,
while we sit
in this boat and row,
aiming at a point on the bank
that gets smaller
as the distance gets shorter.

2

Above us, scraggy clouds
chased across the sky
by a crazy chinook wind.
The water skittish and factious,
and late birds
flitting over the waves.
People flaked out on the bank
like weary summer flies
as we push off from the jetty,
long before the storm.

3

The water looks like grass,
gray grass, grasped by the root.

94

TÜBINGEN, IN JANUARY

for Georg Braungart

The sky snowless,
in the vines' rigging
the day comes to light.
Dead-tired, last year's wood,
goes to work before me.
Time wasted and beaten,
how useless the language.
It may seem strange to you,
but even crows have a heart.
And that is, in a few words,
the true story of my life.

ABOUT SHADOW

I knew the good and the bad kinds of shadows,
the shapeless shadow of dreams in which theologians
argue about splitting hairs, and the shadow
cast by fish and busy flies.
My grandfather mixed shadow in with grain,
so that something useful would grow
and the chaff would not separate from the wheat.
And once I saw the shadows of birds that
clung to the stones like sheep wool on a bush.
From today even my sleep casts a shadow
into a world without light.

BY THE SEA

1

Tiny fires on the shore,
they're burning letters.
Love letters,
undated and incomprehensible.
A kiosk, painted blue,
behind it the slate-gray sea,
in front a money-grubbing chair.
We sense the horizon shifting
its ground even without us.
We sit like this, face one another,
the sea and me,
each a dark mirror
to the other,
and are not allowed to speak.

2

Saint Francis, so they say,
could live for a week
on the clitter of the cicada.
And each day I listen
to the bellow of the waves.

3

Can those be gulls
above the dark juniper
close to the open graves?
Once there were storks here,
they kept the *Book of the Dead*,
and the air was still pure
over the sea.

WATER SKATERS

The sky: a river of granite,
and you start when birds
emerge from the mass
and, gliding in great arcs,
trace their circles round you.
The flawlessness confounds you.

I am rooted to this river bank,
watching fish as they leap,
blithely, out of the water.
In an hour all will be dark.
Now I see the water skaters
staring into the ink-black depths.

Like microscopes they stand on the surface,
motionless, in an hour they'll be dead.

THE BIRDS

The birds in my garden
keep a travelbook.
Sometimes they fly
to the threshold of pain
and bring back names
too heavy for the wind
that keeps them aloft.
I gather them up
and lay them out
like breadcrumbs
for the birds.
In the evening, after sundown,
the travelbook is empty,
as if they had never flown.

THE CROWS OF CORBARA
for H. B.

1

At the end the wishlists get smaller
and the trembling hand
is barely legible by the time you concede
that choosing one path means
turning your back on the others.
It is still the same hand
that once held all our wishes,
the nameless ones and those set
on making the world look different,
as when you step outside after
endless rain and feel at home.
Why does it take so long to realize
that we don't matter?
And why does nobody tell us?
We used to lay coins on the rails
and watch the trains hurtle over them;
now, on its own, the image wears away.

2

I don't know what I should wish for.
Perhaps to make my way to Corbara again,
where a landwind bends the leaves
of olive trees towards the sea and sets
the cypresses nodding like drowsy nannies,
or where it shakes the melancholy pines
until the crows fall into the thin shadow
that politely covers the path—that path,
that shines at night if we take care
to leave no tracks on our way to the sea.
Yes, the crows of Corbara belong half
to the land and half to the sea, above the cliff
they make material the balance of the world.
And we, with our nose for what is false, stand
there, honest and fragile, and gawp in disbelief.

3

The sea and I, we understand each other better.
A worn shoe lies on the shore and a track
goes back into the whispering surf. We insist

on the visible and will not attend to the
whispering, secretive languages.
A great flood from the black granite of the sea
fills me and scatters the many words for unhappiness.
And then the crows above Corbara, their hoarse-throated caw.

GNOSTIC EXERCISE, CORSICA

In the pines the crows' secret council,
gray vests over black robes,
at issue: the flies that must perish,
for the world to be just once more.

On the agenda of dawn:
the transformation of stones into light.
You do not ask of grass why
it bows to the whims of the wind,

or stones to give up their age.
Straggling dune grass, your stammer
is the true sign of redemption,
not to be had without you.

A cross, made of light, is brought
to the shore by the sheep.
October. The cycle of the year
has spared these things:

the shoe, the bottle, the torn shirt,
they all lie there waiting for redemption.
A dog drives the breakers back,
they carry the letters with them

that were busy forming a word.
Arcadia, exile, respite.
I read the story of Ben Asi,
who glimpsed the secret of paradise

and died.

LATE SEPTEMBER

1

Heavy clouds in a September sky
and the ground stretches to take them in,
the houses straighten up, a sycamore,
heavy with night, opens its hands,
and the brackish stream, only now
dragging like a prisoner, murmurs
hope to itself in the morning.

2

Then, quiet, and time is inside me,
dreams the dreams of the dead,
unabashed by the life that runs aground.

3

So it was that truth wandered
into my house, erased the scribble,
and eased the pain for an hour or so,
then settled on the heap of wreckage
that night had left behind for me.

4

Only the cats refuse to be fooled.
They creep in and out as if the house,
too, stood in ruins.

UZBEKISTAN NIGHTS

In front of the President's palace
a few shame-faced trees
stand watch over the dust.
Women with eyes the color of dates
selling nuts, all nuts
belong to the nation.
And everything is true and false.

A FRIEND SPEAKS

I had forgotten Berlin, now
I see it with different eyes.
The din of cars on the cobbled streets
before dawn, like beets being chopped.
And the jet trails, as then,
that mimic the lines of my hand,
as if they had studied my fate.
What was the name of that neighbor,
the collector of worn-out words, words
with no clue what would come, unprepared
for the misery they would have to express?
His house still stands, foxes live in the garden,
as if that were normal in days like these.
I study the atlas of clouds,
the gift of a benevolent heaven,
before it bade its farewells.

IN BULGARIA
for Penka Angelova

The brown and white pigeons of Ruse
haul the dusk over the river,
and in the sandbanks where the anglers grow,
the gulls are building a house out of dust,
as if things like that still mattered.
On the hill a mulberry tree.
Every twig, every leaf draws me
into a Cyrillic exchange about water.
I still don't know what I'm looking for.
People sleep in watermelons,
they squeeze the seeds from their eyes.
Only the children here never sleep,
but follow the water into an arid land.

SOFIA, IN FEBRUARY

Clear weather on the way to Sofia.
From above a nice view of the
columns of smoke, the first sign of wars.

The plane shakes itself over the Balkans,
but history maintains its equilibrium.
Mr. Goes-without-Saying sleeps next to me.

As we approach we see Boyadzhiev's crow-trees,
they give the sorry sky a glow.
(If you want to know how beauty comes into being!)

I buy a paper I can't even read,
share my money with a gypsy.
At every corner I catch sight of myself,

and then the real Bulgaria begins.

NORTHERN CEMETERY, MUNICH

Gossiping stones.
Only one grave
can lock up the tale.
When a forget-me-not
steps in
and talks death
into the blue.

CONSTRUCTION PIT

Not a squeak from heaven these days,
sullen clouds, silent afternoons,
a sickly and lily-livered light.
And now and again—face turned away—
a breeze that stumbles heedlessly
over the crossing like a sleepwalker.

Outside my window the pit,
where everything comes to rest: cracked
bricks, a doll with teeth smashed in,
insomniac rubbish and a bike that's been
digging its way into the earth for days.
Not a clue who it was dug out the pit.

Sometimes you see men down there,
they look like dwarves, testing the
rain-soaked walls with thin fingers.
One of them has a pocket mirror,
he's trying to catch the clouds.
You hear him day and night swearing.

He will become my neighbor, later,
when I've run out of words
for the light.

MEETING ON A TRAIN

Unbidden he sets out
the important things in life.
A few books that put
the wind in his sails,
a love
he couldn't show,
whatever the cost;
the oracles of thunder;
setting suns;
the smell of fresh wood;
a map without borders
as big as his hand;
good diplomatic relations
with all animals, with all;
things that don't mean much
but tell us something;
miniscule gods,
tiny as ants.
And so on, until Cologne.
Almost too much for one life.
And then he gets off
and forgets us.

UNDIGESTED MATERIAL

for Adam Zagajewski

The trees stand round me like
ancient patriarchs, gentle and sad,
rehearsing their orthodox liturgy.
Infinity quivers in every leaf.
Strict, stubborn and thoughtless,
the wind blows through the grass
that puts up with anything.
In truth we've understood nothing.
They say no story can be lost,
only its kernel of wisdom
is fugitive, out on the loose.
The worst is already behind us,
one of those secrets, out at last,
that we must speak about,
the rest is
what we've forgotten.
What can never be finished.

LATE SUMMER

I stood a long time in the shade
under the scabby branches of the linden.
The tin roof of the shed
creaked in the heat,
and the raspberries, sprayed by the fox,
gave off faint signals:
you mustn't pick us.
Late summer caught mid-flight
stared at me, wheatened.
Why are there good reasons
not to despise what is bad?
I took load after load
off my mind and gave it
to the little gods playing cards
in the grass and touting for business.
I stood there so long the mist
snatched away my legs and I
had no clue where I should
search for myself.

THE PATH

A quiet evening. I walk slowly,
watching the path, the short path,
pass me by, towards its end.
The gray grief of the beech trees.
A will that stood fast for years
has been broken and the gravel
under my feet no longer resembles
that hard scree that once
lay here. Grasshoppers
with freshly ironed wings
and butterflies like faint smoke
over the fresh-mown grass.
My grandfather knew when and how
to make the cut, so that new life began
and the conversation did not end
when he had to leave the garden.
Black as a mole, a thunderstorm
gathers over the hillside,
the path carries on undeterred.

SIMULTANEITY

Weather: healthy,
and over the wooden fence
the chatter of raspberries.
My true love gives up
her little ring to the magpies
and dies.
Then at once the flight
of crows begins
in the unquiet light
and the heart of the naked lady
blooms the summer
out.

2009

for Remco Campert

The harvest concludes
in the measure of summer,
the wind speaks softly
with the call of the crows.
The slender-shouldered birch,
dictates its diary to the haggard light:
today I carried a hawk!

Nothing can be restored. The evening
no longer transforms into knowing.
We choose the forgotten paths,
where we are greeted only by stones
and each one tries hard to remember,
as though it would be nothing without us.
I wanted to tell you this
before you hear it from others.

EMPTY RIVERBED

Just like those rivers that make off
out of their beds and leave behind
a pile of hapless stones,
we stand on the oldest morning
before papers covered with scribble
and try to crack the secret code.
The stones write history too.
It's just a case of setting them down,
so that later, when the thaw comes, the script
can be seen under the ferment of water.

HALFLIGHT

A little fox crosses the road
and reddens the edge of the forest.
Beyond it the broken earth of the fields
as if someone had wanted to get in.
No way back to the bend,
where the little fox vanished.
I ought to turn round, now,
but my ignorant hand,
will not permit the maneuver,
as if I had sworn an oath,
to see truth and pass it by.

MOSQUITO

One might think it exaggerated
to raise a memorial for a midge.
But it too, through my blood,
has its part in the primal history of fear.

ANONYMOUS LETTER

Someone sends me photos,
they show us: him and me.
And a story that unfolds,
without my understanding,
as if I stood accused
in some old trial.
A story plucked from the history
of misery that has a point to make:
I did not want to be who I was
and do not want to be who I am.
In the background a girl,
spindly and blonde, with scabs
on her funny knees, staring
straight into the sky, not
into a vanishing life.

UMBERTO SABA'S GOAT

If you were to ask me
my favorite animal,
I would say Saba's goat,
with the Trotzkyite beard.
That's how I imagine the angel
stepping out of the darkness.
We first met on the Karst,
where the wind weighs no more
than shadow.
She believed in the honeysuckle shoots,
I plumped for the immutable grass.
We exchanged some correspondence,
her address an abandoned stall.
Sometimes we encounter one another
in tattered anthologies.
She comes after the crickets,
I'm with the crows.
Between us a void
that can never be filled.

LAST TRAIN

Someone approached me slowly,
hat pulled down,
hand shading his eyes,
an off-duty poet.
On his T-shirt the words:
I speak the language of Paradise.
He walked right through me
and took the last train,
the one meant for me.
No idea, what became
of me. Of the truth
we know only the miserable gist.

THE JUG

Fill the jug for me,
the blue one with white spots,
put a drop of sorrow in
a scrap of sleep
and a little bit of love
and the dust of grief,
for we mustn't forget the dust!
And put it in the window,
closest to the sun,
for a honey-bright moment.

STILL LIFE

Matches, burned out,
and shoes that don't want to go
out of fashion.
The curtain blows brightly to the West.
From the cloisters of night,
voices unheard.
And again your calls are fewer,
your mouth grows thinner,
mortified.

GENEALOGY

1
On the Lenzheide moor
I killed a mosquito.
One of its ancestors accompanied
Nietzsche on his way to the Engardin.

2
A cow grazes in front of the house,
the last in a line of cows.
One of its ancestors, brown and white,
was served up to Napoleon
shortly before he met Goethe in Weimar.

110

LATE READINGS

The storm tears at the shutters,
as if it wanted to steal the light
that my words work to produce,
my hemisphere of dreams.
A war that goes on too long
cannot be won.
At some lines it just falls asleep.
And yet we kept on believing,
we unbelievers, that we had
nothing to fear from heaven.
The pine tree, upright by day,
like some inquisitor general,
buckles and writes its
confession in the grass.
To be open. To stay open,
a river's mouth,
endlessly renewing itself
in different languages.
If things were other, we would
not have been cast out of paradise.

AFTER THE RAIN

A dog drags a trembling life
across the street, a child carries his god
in a plastic bag under his jacket,
the crows make out they're theologians.
After the rain the world becomes other.
The river is rolling towards me,
shouting so loud I'll go under.
A storm, they say, waits in the books.
We'll read them after the rain,
if there is to be any After-the-Rain.

MY TALISMAN

My talisman is a tiny mouse,
much smaller than everyday mice.
She eats what I eat. She's made of wood.
By day she gnaws at beauty,
by night at my heart.
I can hear her heart beating.
If it's true that in death
one retrieves all one's former faces,
my last face will think of her.

SURPRISE VISIT

The doorbell. A woman asking
for coins for the eyes
of her dead daughter.
I give her two nuts
from my nut trees,
one from each tree.
Where the canopies meet
a dense tympanum forms,
and at the center a blackbird
sits with its olive-green eyes.
The woman takes the nuts
and leaves—and I, in panic,
run back to my book
on the subject of "outer space,"
so as not to forget its tongue.

LITTLE CHURCH

Sometimes, in little churches,
you want to thank the paintings
for still being there: Lazarus,
growing out of the saltpeter,
like a bright blister, and Jonah,
no idea where he's got caught;
saints, who dish up their dreams
and martyrs who've risked their necks.
There is no redemption, they whisper,
but you too will have a second life.
Swallows scatter the light
that would otherwise fall into darkness
and from outside you hear the cock.
You couldn't really hope for more
stepping out into the blissful night.
A second life?
No coming over pious out of weakness, now!
the paintings call after you.

ON THE MOORS, IN MARCH

When misery has you in its claws,
there's no place more desolate.
The stunted birches have founded an order
no one wants to join, and the ground
groans as though it had lost its mind.
What goes under here will always survive.
It's how I, prisoner of childhood,
imagine paradise after the fall.

DOG

I love shady pathways
and the park round the corner,
where the dossers talk about God and the world.
They can call me dog,
I've recently lost my
worldly name.
It pleases me to be nameless again
among the houses and people.
God, said a poor wretch the other day,
has dished out too many names,
and lost track of what there is.
Dog.
Only I know what is behind it.

HOTEL ROOM

As I enter the room, still in my coat,
without hope of wisdom or sleep,
all the rooms I have ever slept in
are already gathered to greet me.
The sorry wallpaper, a history of art
from its worst side, the sofa
with whole novels alive in its cracks.
The lackluster Bible bound in plastic,
dog-eared at all the difficult verses.
Not least the implacable mirror
that refuses to recognize me.
The dead stand at the door.
They do nothing. They are waiting.
Don't worry, they whisper,
this life, too, will soon have been endured.

THE SPIDER

Outside the house the children play
crazy, as if there were only
friend or foe. I think
of a groundless piety,
inaccessible to prayer.
In a corner of the room a spider
works at a fair copy of nature.
When it has made its web,
childhood will come to an end.

CONCERNING GRACE

The word grace goes
from phrase to phrase begging
admittance in vain.
Coarser, harder words
have taken the seats
and are performing
a piece called reality,
a tragedy, without an interval
but a raft of rave reviews.
A play about lonely words.

SAECULUM OBSCURUM

Huge clouds from the south,
a monumental folktale
from which blurred shadows
fall to earth.
Alexander had his head
engraved on hard coins,
always the same profile,
an impression of truth.
In the woods they're rehearsing
the sermon to the birds,
that's where we belong.

PUB IN THE SUBURBS

The situation is obscure,
two strip-lights cast no shadow,
a child turning the wheel of emptiness,
he's seen through me.
The barman an Arab. He tells
the story of Muhammad
who hid behind a spider's web.
There are midnight-blue spirits
meant to trick the Qur'an.
Then a song. And everyone stands up
and cries.

DAILY NEWS

Germany has run out of money,
and it's our job, says the announcer,
to claw it back, even if it takes
three generations. In any case
the sun goes down at 19.07 tonight.
Murder and mayhem on all
five continents, the oldest woman
in Japan has bitten the dust
and taken the whole world with her.
At 19.10 it's pitch black.

DEATH OF THE POET

The filthy yard,
between the words, the weeds.
The forest behind with its furrowed profile.
A light in the house of the dead man,
furious moths at the window,
they want to pay their respects.
By the door letters and papers,
with news on the front page
of the death of the poet, so the ants
read who it is being mourned.

ABOUT CHILDHOOD

When childhood came to an end,
wonder was finished too.
I stood, surely only yesterday,
at the field's edge, where poppies
and daisies told me fables.
I stared with my hand over my eyes
after the setting sun.
In the linden tree, older than war
and older than peace,
hung the *Bürgermeister*, listening,
head down, to the bees.
He'd not meant it to turn out like this.

FAIR COPY

We have reconstructed my childhood
with ordinary things.
A pine cone, bread crumbs,
keys, a black-veined stone,
anything to hand and easily carried.
It's just that things have a habit
of acting as they see fit,
and the course I wanted to steer
keeps veering out of control.
I see what I no longer am,
but I cannot see myself.
An apple rolls sadly from the table
and breaks as words break
when they're not used for a while.
Leave it to the birds to
fair copy this scribble, on them
one can rely.

Karen Leeder

from *Time to be Changed*
2013

HOW POEMS COME INTO BEING

Everyone knows that moment
stepping out into a clearing,
when the hares,
after a second's hesitation,
disappear in the undergrowth.
There is not a word
that could keep them.
You're out of your mind,
my father would say,
when tears welled in my eyes.
How should one imagine a whole,
if one does not know
what wholeness is.

CROW-BITER

"Crows," says a man
who has lived through the war,
"should only be cooked
on pinewood,
to absorb the poisons.
And eaten with sorrel,
which livestock avoids."
Incomprehensible the order
of the world in peacetime.
We sit in the open, marvel
at the setting sun.
The crows in the pine tree
have the last word.

I DON'T KNOW IF THERE'S A REASON

In the woods I came across blackberries,
growing entwined with lamellar variegated ivy
that cloaked a ruin, a crumbling wall,
on which there hung a bell. It was hot from the sun.
I pressed the button, in jest, to be fair.
At once a group of gods crossed the clearing,
in no great hurry and deep in conversation,
one of them hung back, wanting to be alone.
What nonsense the gods talk. If I'm not mistaken,
we'll soon know the exact date of our death,
I heard one of them say, it is already written.
I heard it correctly, didn't want to understand.

WOODHOUSE
for Alfred Kolleritsch

You must stand with your back
to the wall, in the evening light.
Then you will see the storm,
announcing itself in the crown
of the linden. The blackbirds are frantic,
as if this had to do with late work.
You will be measured by how often
you have not told the truth—though the word
was warm on the tip of your tongue.
One glance at the clouds chasing past
and the breach between the heavenly
and the earthly world is clear.
Your back against the warmth of wood,
and then the sun goes down.

JOY

How the lupine smells,
the yarrow after rain,
the knotweed, that won't
relinquish the stone.
It takes too long
before you are sent back
into childhood,
when words had the time
to reveal their wealth.
A late understanding
acquired through weakness.
If you were to show
me a field bean now,
I'd drop down dead
with joy.

LAST DAY IN AUGUST

The apple tree is bowed
with the weight of the crop, soon
it will fling the fruit into the grass
because I haven't picked them yet.
There is no wind, and yet
a single leaf begins
spinning like a lunatic.
Something isn't right.
Even songbirds are dumb.
What we, after long deliberation,
call the density of life
puts words into doubt,
language falls short.
Now the density is mute
and the apple lies not so far from the tree.

DEATH OF THE BIRCH TREE, 2011

First it was a fungus growing
from its hip, a fleshy wedge,
then a gust of wind stole its leaves
and let them fall without care,
finally it lost its color.
That's how I imagine the end,
the little diminutions ahead of time.
Today the tree gave way.
The stone that stood at its foot
refuses to lose face.
A new calendar begins:
year one after the death of the birch.

MEMORY OF SCHOOL

One girl spoke of nothing but acacia,
she was crazy for its scent.
She knew Pliny by heart,
Horace she adored,
Boethius she thought a god.
But when the acacia was blossoming,
nothing could stand in her way.
I can't remember her name.

POEM

I could talk about wars,
about gods who invented
life out of boredom, about hedgehogs
in my garden, about me.
I could talk about someone
who studies the variant readings of misery
like a Romanian philosopher.
Laurel, too,
serves to ward off demons.
But best play dumb,
the silence is loud enough.

IN THE NEGEV

for N. C.

I have seen how the bear
hugs the shield of its enemy,
and the lion, in the shade
of the tamarisk, finishes its prey.
The hunt as savory knowledge.
I have counted the Negev
sand, the glorious sand,
that cannot keep hold of my tracks.

HOTEL NEAR ERFURT

Only the dead stay here,
they pay their bill with ashes.
You see their shadows
at the windows,
the shadows of children, too.
The taxi driver told me
about a mathematician
from Jena, who died in '45,
and knew the exact number
of all the dead here on earth.
No one is lost.
No luggage allowed,
if you want to move in.
Even books are forbidden.

ILLUMINATION

Standing like this,
the sea gives me
a light
that sets me on fire, and with my feet
I can read
the braille of the pebbles.

SHAME

June light. A late visitor
peeled himself from the dark of the hedge
and spoke in the childlike language
of twigs. Farmer-like,
cap over his eyes.
He was true to bats, he said,
praised the catechism of creatures,
but loved above all the clowning
of butterflies before they died of cold.
We sat on the bench in front of the house
and watched the raindrops
filling and falling.
Then he was gone, the late storyteller,
leaving behind only his name,
an unpronounceable name.
All those stories of his, I could
have told them myself, I thought,
but said nothing out of shame.

CINNAMON

Suddenly someone hits upon
cinnamon, as if it were to blame
for all the secret compacts
between heaven and earth: cinnamon.
My grandmother had four sticks
tucked away from before war, that's all.
The birch tree shakes off winter,
the wind tests how soundly it stands.
And all I do is think of cinnamon.
Call the moon a pumpkin,
for all I care,
but when someone says cinnamon,
I feel only the warmth of the dead.

LOST TIME

The taxi comes too late, the bus
cannot wait, and the plane
refuses, for technical reasons,
to leave solid ground. You know
how it is, stomach is empty,
deep, dark, unshakable,
lost time. Public telephones,
a thing of the past. Besides,
I wouldn't have known how to explain.
So many words, one says simply
to be rid of them. Spit it out!
Strange taxis and buses speeding
past you, planes crossing overhead,
their trails drift towards the place
your story was meant to arrive.
One half of the sky is on fire.
A beginning, that has no beginning,
an end without end, and a bolt from the blue
that rips through time like old paper.

ISTANBUL REVISITED

for Sezer Duru

Thirty years on I went back to visit
the cistern carp of Istanbul.
That first time a tanker had burned
in the Bosporus, the 'Independenţa,'
as I recall. Like a rusty tortoise
gasping for air to fan the flames,
and young Anatolian soldiers
with automatic rifles were clearing
the smoke that hung black over the city,
and left everyone speechless.
I can still see the thick coils of cable
across the streets, dotted with crows,
that, by order of the secret police,
listened in to the whispered talk about
the price of lamb, love and work in Germany.
The owl called the watch from Afrasiab's towers,
and the spider spun curtains for the palace of the Caesars.
Then I saw the carp again in the sunken cistern
of Istanbul; since the time of Justinian
they've been predicting the fate of the empire.
With the passion of the gravid they haul
their gloom over the mossy stones,
my ancient brothers, they know everything
and yet do nothing, they don't even look up
when a coin from Europe grazes their back.
Some of them lie, morose and dark, like inlay
in the depths, bottom-feeding, reading
the *Historia Arcana* for news of the Barbarian invasion.
What saves them is the retreating light.

ADRIAN DIEL

The Diel's butter pear
we owe to him,
the form and taste of
the liver-red Himbeerapfel
he described more precisely
than art historians the still lives
of the Dutch masters.
Color and texture of the flesh,
place and culture of the soil,
the great English Renette
kept him occupied for years.
Everything had been researched,
only the classification of fruit trees
had not found its Homer before him.
My apple tree
has started to bear fruit again, all of them
inedible and good.

CZESŁAW MIŁOSZ

The year had started so well.
I was able to visit St. Roch
the animal healer, while at the other end
of the street, civil wars broke out
and their blood seeped across the TV screen.
The tiny doorway of memory, so long
closed, suddenly opened a chink,
and I saw myself in the middle of Venice,
sitting on a bench, that was reserved
for death. Women wandered past,
whispering their secrets, on the way
to the boat or off to the station,
and then Miłosz came up to me,
walking stick behind his back, a net
in his hand filled with glittering fish.
You couldn't really tell that he was dead,
as he stood there reciting poems,
the way some people talk of rising prices
for truth, for vegetables and fruit.

WHAT IS STILL TO BE DONE
for Peter Handke on his 70th birthday

Gather the nuts
before the squirrel finds them;
bring the shadow in safely,
have words with the pencil
when it ignores what we say;
no longer wish to find the enemy
lurking in our unthought thoughts;
scour the clouds to read
the never-ending epos
about form and transformation;
lift the stone from your forehead;
give astonishment a moment of grace.

And don't forget: to look for the place
where the book has gone missing,
the book with the empty pages,
the empty book, the book.

CLAUDE SIMON

Claude Simon sat down
next to me in a dream,
face all green.
By mistake he'd
eaten meatballs
at the Wannsee in Berlin.
I took his tiny hands
and hauled him back
into real life.
We drank his wine,
a red from Provence,
and read from the Georgica
that he wanted to rewrite
after the war.
"Refusing to make anything real,"
he didn't say much more,
though talking was never his strong point.
"Do you see that butterfly?"
he asked, as he was leaving,
"Odysseus, who doesn't want to go home."
That's when I awoke.

WHO DUNNIT?

In last year's honey
a fly
is preserved intact.
The perfect murder.
Detective novels
could begin like that
or finish.

APPLES IN FEBRUARY

Apples still hang in the bare branches,
they've been spared by the frost
that came from the South overnight,
and, with its raw bite, sealed the land,
the garden, the view of the garden,
and the heart that once dreamed of snow.
And what apples! Skins burst open
and brown, half-eaten flesh,
that even blackbirds refuse.
Awful, sad: as though the war
that we'd been told would come in Spring
had already passed through.
I stood and looked, until I could see
nothing that compared with these poor apples.

SUCKERS

Today our two agaves were
brought home after spending
the winter in a greenhouse
at the nursery round the corner,
along with the elegant plants
sought after in our neighborhood.
I thought they would have slept
and dreamed of Mexico or the Levant,
of tired mules and the quiet
after the bombing had stopped.
The opposite is true.
Under their bright green fleshy spikes
we see more than twenty suckers peeping
out, eager and curious like kittens.
Do you want rid of them? the gardener
asks, he smells of moldy wool.
They will either burst the terracotta pot
or the lot of them will die.
I am now sixty-eight years old
and cannot make the decision.
By the end of October, we will know more.

AT THE SEA, NEAR BOSTON

The wind, tired of the thorny hedges,
has finally dropped—
Be still now, too, sea!
The morning cold as ashes.
Even the insects abandon
their heathen handiwork.
Breathing seems like
an invention
one has not yet mastered.
There's not much to be seen
of God in this light.

BY THE BALTIC, VERY EARLY

1

Like restless sandpipers
that follow their tracks
from the previous day.
Like grasses that cast no shadow.

Children, tired from sleeping,
snarl at the sea.

It took a long time
for the Emperor's message
to wash up here.
But now no one cares what it says.

2

Empty snail shells, mussels.
The good always looks much better than it is,
the bad, as ever, far too eloquent.

POSTCARD, MAY 2012

The door to the terrace stands open,
the yellow march of the dandelions
slowly takes over the lawn.
The squirrel is looking for nuts
from last year. They say it will rain,
the swing already dreams of the wind.
If those fat Sunday papers
are right, none of this exists.
Not the woodpecker busy confiding
its elegy to the sycamore, and not
the weeds, friend to the bumblebee.
Because we despise imperfection,
an invisible machine now works
at perfection. Besides,
even the apple tree that, like me,
came into the world at a time of war,
has started to flower again.

CLEARING

1

The drama of leaves
falling; and you,
far away, at pains
to read a world where no one
understands farewell,
turning back halfway
between eye and heart.

2

Leaves weep for the dead,
only the sparrows, unconcerned,
can be bought off with crumbs.
The world to come,
looked at through cruel eyes,
will find its beginning
in the willing hearts of words.

3

Everything trembles.
And God trembles too.

Contents

DIDEROTS KATZE

NACHTS, UNTER BÄUMEN

KURZ VOR DEM GEWITTER

UNTER FREIEM HIMMEL

INS REINE

UMSTELLUNG DER ZEIT

DIDEROTS KATZE

VOR DEM ESSEN. VIER UHR FRÜH
für Fred Oberhauser

Sie habe noch nie allein gegessen, ganz für sich,
noch nie habe sie das Gefühl gehabt, selbständig
eine Mahlzeit zu sich zu nehmen. Zuerst die Mutter.
sagte sie, vor dem Eisschrank stehend, die nicht nur

neben ihr stand, ihr den Löffel führte, die bestimmte,
wie und was und wieviel gegessen wurde, sondern auch
im Essen selber war. Ich habe nur gegessen, um der
Mutter zu gefallen. Sie war nicht nur im Essen, in

den Speisen, sie war zunehmend das Essen selber.
Meine Mutter, sagte sie, vor dem offenen Eisschrank,
im Nachthemd und frierend, war sozusagen die Speise,
die ich täglich aß. Daher ihre Magerkeit, behauptete

sie, ihre Unfähigkeit, Essen bei sich zu behalten;
ihre Unempfindlichkeit besonderen Speisen gegenüber.
In Restaurants z. B. das Gefühl, in einem Museum zu
sein, das Gefühl, außerhalb der natürlichen Ordnung

sich zu befinden: ihre Gier in Restaurants, die Manie,
alles bestellen zu wollen, und die trostlose Gewiß-
heit, nichts von den Gerichten essen zu können. Ihre
Euphorie angesichts miserabler Gerichte in Gast-

häusern: ob ich das bemerkt hätte. Ich hatte nicht
vor, etwas zu antworten. Die hoffnungslose Einsamkeit
beim Essen, während des Eßvorgangs, besonders bei
fetten Leuten, ob mir das auch aufgefallen sei, der

Versuch, sich ganz auszufüllen und das Mißlingen
solcher Versuche. Auch die Unfähigkeit, sämtliche
Gerichte in eine Ordnung zu bringen, das käme ihr
vor wie im Museum: die Freßgier verdanke sich einem

Ordnungswillen, aber eben einem nicht zu befriedigenden
Ordnungswillen, dafür sprächen auch die aufgerissenen
Augen, die nach einem System suchen, natürlich nicht
finden. Ich zum Beispiel kann nicht mit geschlossenen

Augen essen, sagte sie, die Vorstellung, nicht zu sehen,
was ich esse, ruft Schwindelanfälle hervor, die Peri-
staltik versage augenblicklich, auch wenn sie gesehen
habe, wie der Ober die Speisen gebracht habe, daß er

sie gebracht habe. Sie fror. Du bist mager geworden in
den letzten Jahren, sagte ich. In Krisensituationen, sie, würde
sie jetzt immer zu nehmen: allein die Anwesenheit von
Personen würde sie aufquellen lassen. Jeder mache un-

bewußt den Versuch, sie vollzustopfen, eine Abgabe,
eine Abnahme sei undenkbar in derartigen Situationen:
sie fühle sich dann ganz offen. (Und früher?) hätte sie
sofort abgenommen, hätte sich sozusagen verstreut,

alles sei früher aus hinausgeflossen: spürbar.
Sie hätte förmlich sehen können, wie alles aus ihr
hinausgeflossen sei. Früher sei sie in Krisen-
situationen sofort dünn wie ein Strich geworden. Wie

jetzt, sagte ich. Plötzlich war es draußen hell geworden.
Der Kühlschrank stand immer noch offen, es war sehr kalt.
Dir ist kalt, sagte ich. Die Eßvorgänge, die Eßmoral,
die früheren Erregungszustände beim Essen würden ihr

jetzt, in der Erinnerung, einen kalten Schauder den
Rücken hinunterjagen, sagte sie; sie sei in die Küche
geschlichen, um Essen zu lernen, auch wenn das sonderbar
klänge. In Krisensituationen sein Gewicht behalten,

das wäre ideal. Ich möchte in Krisensituationen
mein Gewicht behalten, sagte sie, deshalb bin ich hier.
Ich möchte nichts abgeben und ich möchte nichts auf-
nehmen, ich möchte unangreifbar sein und sehr rund. Das

sei die einzige Möglichkeit, behauptet sie, zitternd
vor Kälte. Ein rund gläserner Körper, in dem sie den
Vorgang des Verdauens beobachten könne, den Vorgang des

Zersetzens und Ausscheidens, ohne daß sich der Körper
verändere: sie sei auf dem besten Wege dahin. Es sei
ihr unbegreiflich, daß man so wenig Interesse für diese
Vorgänge habe. Warum, fragte sie mich, wurde das verlernt?
Ich stellte sämtliche Herdplatten an und begann mit den

Vorbereitungen. Diderot, sagte ich, beim Kartoffelschälen,
hat es auf dem Totenbett nach Kartoffeln verlangt, ein
polemischer Wunsch in der Geschichte der Zivilisation.

NACHGEDICHT

Die Zeichen sprechen
eine andere Sprache:

das ist ihr gutes Recht.
Wir haben uns zu fest
auf ihre Zweideutigkeit
verlassen,

jetzt sind wir beleidigt
und schweigsam. Schon wieder

sitzen wir fest
auf fremden Stühlen und wühlen
ergeben in Papierbergen. Vieles
reimt sich wieder,

was uns vor ein paar Jahren
wie ein Versprecher vorkam.

ARCHÄOLOGIE

1

Das ganze Jahr über ('75) wollte ich
ein politisches Gedicht schreiben über

Deutschland; es sollte Die Unnatürliche Wärme
heißen und war gedacht für einen Freund in

Kalifornien, der nicht nach Deutschland
kommen konnte in diesem Jahr, der nicht

durch Deutschland reisen konnte in diesem
Jahr, um die Veränderungen selber zu sehen:

das Gedicht sollte die Lücke füllen
zwischen seinem letzten Aufenthalt hier

und dem nächsten, damit er nicht erschrickt
und sofort zurückfährt das nächste Mal

oder hastig auf seinem Ticket nachschauen
muß, ob er in einem anderen Land gelandet

ist, etwa. Das ganze Jahr über sammelte ich
Material für Die Unnatürliche Wärme über

die unnatürlich Wärme, die sich ausgebreitet
hat über Deutschland: in den Zeitungen und

Zeitschriften, den Wohnungen und auf der
Straße, in den Köpfen und in der Rede über

die große Kälte, die sich ausgebreitet haben
soll in den Zeitschriften und Zeitungen,

auf der Straße und in den Wohnungen, in der
Rede und in den Köpfen. Pünktlich jeden Ersten

setzte ich mich hin und sichtete das Material
für mein meteorologisches Gedichte: die Notizen

über den Wind, der uns mit plötzlicher Heftigkeit
ins Gesicht bläst; über das rasch sich ausbreitende

Tief und den damit zusammenhängenden Wetterum-
schwung; über die kalte Meeresluft, die aus Südwest-

europa kommt und nach Nordosten fließen soll;
über die Klimaschwankungen und sonstigen meteoro-

logischen Einbrüche. Ich wollte versuchen, die sich
ausbreitende Angst vor der angekündigten Kälte

zu beschreiben und was die Angst angerichtet hat:
daß alle plötzlich nähe zusammengerückt sind,

um sich zu wärmen; daß alle sich plötzlich
vermummt haben und kaum noch wiederzuerkennen sind;

daß kaum einer mehr auf der Straße zu sehen ist;
daß die wenigen zum Himmel starren und die Forma-

tionen der Wolken interpretieren; daß, als Folge
der Angst vor der angekündigten Kälte, es im Sommer

in Deutschland so aussah als wär schon Dezember. Man
flüstert wie im Winter, hatte ich mir notiert, dabei

brennt die Sonne heißer denn je. Es sollte ein Gedicht
werden über die sich ausbreitende Macht der Meteoro-

logie und ihre nachweislich falschen Prognosen

2

Am Ende des Jahres, am 16. Dezember 1975, wurde mir
der Koffer mit meinen Aufzeichnungen am Flughafen

Tegel gestohlen. Mißmutig saß ich in einem Hotel in
Littlehampton, an der Südküste Englands, Europa

gegenüber, draußen war es kalt und es goß in Strömen,
und überlegte, ob man den Golfstrom umgeleitet

hat aus klimatischen Überlegungen. Ich las unun-
terbrochen deutsche Zeitungen, die mit großer Ver-

spätung eintrafen. Die Archäologie war wiederent-
deckt worden in Deutschland, las ich und dachte unun-

terbrochen an mein Gedicht. So schnell geht die Ziet
vorbei, Donnerwetter. Die Archäologie der Oper. Die

Archäologie des Kinos. Mein großes politisches Gedicht
über Deutschland war beim Teufel. Ich stellte mir

riesenhafte Ausgrabungsstätten vor in Deutschland,
ein vollkommen umgegrabenes Rhein-Main-Gebiet, Baden-

Württemberg ein einziges schwarzes Loch. Die Archäologie
der Zukunft. Auch das vergangene Jahr wurde unter den

verschiedensten archäologischen Gesichtspunkten
beurteilt. Ein merkwürdiges Verfahren. Mein Jahr,

das Jahr meines geplanten Gedichts. Merkwürdigerweise
gab es nur wenig Überschneidungen. In der Beurteilung

des Klimas wichen sämtliche Kommentare von meinen
Beobachtungen ab, z.B. Oder ein anderes Datum, das in

keinem Jahresrückblick berücksichtigt wurde: 1975 war
der Faschismus in Deutschland seit 30 Jahren vorbei. Oder wie?

Stattdessen überall eine lange Liste der Toten; weiß-
haarige Männer und Frauen mit vor Sorge gefurchten

Gesichtern. Ich flog rasch zurück nach Berlin, um
an Ort und Stelle nach meinen Manuskripten zu

forschen: mein geplantes Gedicht würde tatsächlich
eine Lücke füllen im Angebot, wenn es zustandekäme,

dachte ich. Als ich aus dem Flugzeug stieg, wußte
ich: du wirst deine Tasche mit den Aufzeichnungen

nie wiederfinden, nie. Es war saukalt in Berlin,
besonders in der ausgekühlten Wohnung war es kaum

auszuhalten: Eingemummt in Pullover und Decken hockte
ich mich ans Fenster und dachte schlechtgelaunt

nach über den Verlust meines Gedichts und den
seltsamen Aufstieg der Archäologie in Deutschland.

DAS VERBRECHEN

Lehrgedicht zu Brechts 80. Geburtstag

Wir müssen den Fall
der Blätter beschleunigen
Wir riskieren es
Wir müssen den Baum fällen
so schnell wie möglich
Wir riskieren es
Wir brauchen die Erde
darunter dringend
Wir sehen es ein
Wer zögert bedenke:
Die erhabene Natur allein
wird sich dieses Falles erinnern
Wir riskieren den Fall

DIE KATZE IST TOT

Ich fand sie
neben der Mülltonne
steif
nach einem beweglichen Leben.

Seltsam,
sie lag auf dem Bauch
mit ausgetreckten Pfoten.

In dieser Haltung
hatte sie vor mir gelegen
wenn ich ihr vorlesen mußte.

Am liebsten
hörte sie alte Reiseberichte.
Die wahre Geschichte
von Oblomows Weltumseglung
zum Beispiel
kannte sie auswendig.
(Bekanntlich
hatte dieser zaristische Beamte
während der ganzen Fahrt
das Schiff nicht einmal verlassen.)
Das Fremde
zog ihn nicht an,
sagte ich ihr,
wenn sie nachts das Haus noch
verlassen wollte.
Oft
behandelte sie mich
wie ein Kind.

Aber wenn ich mich dann
wie ein Kind benahm
sträubte sie augenblicklich
ihr Fell.

Fehler, Nachlässigkeiten
korrigierte sie
höflich
mit einem Zittern der Schnurrhaare.

Jeder von uns
führte ein Doppelleben
sie in der Nacht
ich tagsüber
das wir streng
voreinander verbargen.

Kürzlich erst
gab sie mir zu verstehen
mich in ihr fellwarmes Leben
einzuweihen

als Belobigung
für geduldiges Beobachten.

Nun starb sie
in der Haltung des Zuhörens.

Und ich fühle mich
als das Opfer.

ERNST MEISTER IN MEMORIAM

In den Dingen
die Augen, Ernst,
noch vor der Sprache.
Gleich, wo du bist,
du kehrst zurück:
Stein, Schwelle, Haus,
du wirst erwartet.
So bleibst du, Ernst,
am Leben,
immer im Blick.

DIDEROTS KATZE

Fotografiert von Gabriele Lorenzer

Diderot am Fenster: neben ihm die Katze,
das schuppige Fell im hellen Rahmen.

Er erklärt ihr den Menschen, die Maschine,
mit brüchiger Stimme: die Elemente
der Physiologie, den Verstand,
die gewaltige Arbeit der Natur.

Er zitiert die Denkschriften
der Akademie der Wissenschaften von 1739,
wo von einem Menschen die Rede ist
ohne Venen und ohne Herz.
Auf Seite 590, fügt er lachend hinzu
und streichelt verlegen das Fell
seiner Katze.

Es gibt Fotografien mit einer längeren Geschichte
als der der Geschichte der Fotografie.

Die Katze beobachtet eine Wolke,
die sich rasch am oberen Fensterdrittel
vorbeibewegt, zu rasch,
und reagiert mit einer panischen Bewegung.
Diderot, abgekämpft nach dreißig Jahren Arbeit
an der Enzyklopädie,
ist sprachlos: der heftige Dialektiker
bewundert die einfache Grammatik
der Nervosität.

Die ganze Seele des Hundes liegt in seiner Schnauze,
sagt er, die ganze Seele des Adlers in seinem Auge,
die des Maulwurfs in seinem Ohr.
Diderot überlegt, ob er weitersprechen soll.

Die Seele des Menschen, beginnt er
– und bricht ab
          (während die Katze
seelenruhig eine Abhandlung über den Einfluß
des Klimas aufs milchige Fensterglas
schreibt);

(während Diderot vor dem Fenster
die Revolution beobachtet, ihre vorsichtigen
Schritte);
ein seltsames Paar:
Diderot und die Katze
im brüchigen Kreuz des Fensters:
seine Angst, ihre Bewegungen nachzuahmen,
ihre sanfte Polemik gegen seine Theorie
der Maschine.

Wir gehen so wenig,
arbeiten so wenig
und denken so viel, sagt Diderot,
daß der Mensch schließlich
nur noch Kopf sein wird.

Es ist Sonntagnachmittag,
eine gute Zeit,
sich an Gefühle zu erinnern;
es ist kalt in Paris
und sehr still;
Diderot spürt, wie schwer es ist,
seine Erfahrungen in Sicherheit zu bringen.

Dreißig Jahre Arbeit an der Enzyklopädie
und noch immer funktioniert die Maschine
schlecht. Vorsichtig prüft Diderot
den Knochenbau seiner Katze.

Wir werden die ersten Barbaren sein,
sagt er plötzlich, die Larmoyanz in seiner Stimme
ist nicht überhörbar.

Meckernd beklagt er das Altern
einer Illusion. Die Katze ist zufrieden.
Mit zusammengekniffenen Augen
betrachtet sie den Staub vor dem Fenster
und kümmert sich einen Dreck
um die Maßlosigkeit der Vernunft.

Diderot gibt sich geschlagen.
Mürrisch schlurft an sein Pult
und notiert:

Woher komme ich?
Was war ich vorher?
Wozu werde ich wieder?
Was für eine Existenz erwartet mich?
Unter welcher Hülle wird mich mein Geschick
wieder hervorbringen?
Das alles weiß ich nicht.

Er läuft zum Fenster
und überlegt, nach einem raschen Blick
auf die Straße.

Erst viel später
nachdem sich die Katze mit einem mächtigen Sprung
aus dem engen Rahmen des Bildes
befreit hat,
fügt er heiter hinzu:

Auch die Philosophie ist eine Anleitung
zum Sterben.

ELEGIE

Bozen, Aussegnungshalle:
kein Wort, das mir Eintritt
verschafft. Ein Schlurfen
spricht sich herum hinter
den Bergen, eine Geschichte
fragt nach dem Weg.

Luft, Luft. Hast du mich
hier erwartet, einen Tag zu spät?
Dein gutes blaues Hemd,
die helle Hose. Wohin
mit deiner Hand, die mich
nicht grüßen kann?

Schnee liegt auf deinem Haar,
laß mich dich wärmen.
Gibt es ein Bild von dir?
Die Zeit hat deinen Körper
ausgewechselt. Du bist
als Fremder mir der beste Freund.

Du mußt zurück
Nach Deutschland, Vater,
auf meine Seite, wo nicht
gesprochen wird vom Tod.
Du lachst? Dein offner Mund
verdächtigt mich. Zu spät.

Wie klein du bist! Doch
wächst der Mensch im Tod
noch um ein Weniges, so wie
der Tod jetzt wächst in uns:
Ein unbescholtner Zeuge
mit hohem Ansehn vor Gericht.

Gefälschter Paß. Schnell,
gib dein Leben, um allem Nachruf
zu entgehn. Zwei Vögel halten Wache
an der Grenze. Und unterm
schwarzen Leib der Wolken
kehrst heimlich du zu uns zurück.

Endlich Erde. Endlich
der Sand in Berlin, hier darfst du
sterben. Schlägst dir den Tod
wie einen Mantel um das Aschenherz –
und gibst dich frei und schweigst:
weil jede Antwort eine Frage wäre.

FUßNOTE

Wir kommen zurück, die Reste
zu holen: Kissen, Überzug, Laken,
eine Zeichnung, die ungeschützt
über dem Herd hing: *Hermes,
der Totengeleiter*, der vier Jahre
lang das Essen würzte. Noch ist Gott
nicht geboren, die Uhr bleibt hängen,
auch der Spiegel im Flur: wie groß
die Wohnung wird, je mehr sie sich
leert, und wie klein die Zeit,
die in den kahlen Zimmern brütet.
Es ist jetzt dunkel, weil wir
die Lampen entfernt haben, alles
geht sanft durch uns hindurch. Dort,
wo früher mein Schreibtisch stand,
versuche ich auf der Wand eine Notiz
zu entziffern: Dein Zorn ist Liebe,
eine Fußnote in der Geschichte
der Eitelkeit, die noch zu schreiben ist.

SKÁCEL

Ihn drängte die Stunde
nach Haus. Noch ein Glas,
eine Zigarette, ein Wort,
das durchs Judentor paßt
mit den flatternden Zungen.
Einmal jährlich erhängt
sich einer, einem andern
fällt die Welt aus der Hand.
Nichts helfen die Verslein
gegen den Tod, den Meister
aus Mähren. Bei uns in Brünn
ist der Schnee wie Staub.
Deine schwarzen Augen
mit den brennenden Brauen,
dein Hemd voller Hecheln.
Noch eine Woche,
dann sehen wir uns,
sechs Tage bist du schon tot.

CAHORS

Einer, nicht angemeldet,
steht im Halbdunkel: läßt
die Stille wachsen
unter umgepflügten Wolken.
Wir begreifen ihn,
seine unsinnige Freude.

Wie unter Bäumen im Winter,
wenn das letzte Blatt,
eben noch Spiegel der Welt,
zur Erde trudelt
und aufschlägt.

Kathedralen wie Bäume.
Eng an den Stamm geschmiegt,
uneingeladen, steht einer
und entziffert die Äste.

156

EIN BRIEF AUS ROM

1

An einem hellen Morgen
im Februar lag roter dichter Sandstaub
auf den Fensterbrettern, wahrscheinlich
aus Afrika, vielleicht aus Tunesien,
von einem empfindlichen Wind hier
abgelegt in Rom. Ein seltenes Ereignis
im Februar, das ich feiern wollte.
Ich schrieb auf die drei Fensterbretter,
wie man mit dem Finger in den Sand
schreibt: eine weiche Kalligraphie
voller Rundungen, die irgendwann
von einem milden Regen zerstört sein wird.

2

Irgendwann. Es war ein Gedicht
über das kleine Stücke Wüste in uns,
über den Sand, den wir lebenslang
zählen in der schweifenden Hoffnung
auf Wissen, über die zahllosen Kopien
und die unzählbaren Wiederholungen.
Die Schlußzeile hieß: Meine Angst
schwieg und meine Sorge verwehte.
Mein Zeigefinger brannte, aber ich
empfand keinen Schmerz: der Text
war geschrieben, kein milder Regen
würde ihn je wieder finden.

3

Und du weißt, es regnete viel
in diesem Februar in dieser Welt
aus bröckelndem Stein, die den Text
auf die Probe stellte. Und uns.
Der Himmel war eine unsaubere Quelle.
Doch nichts ließ mich an der Verbindung
zweifeln zwischen dem roten Sand,
der das dunkle Meer überflogen hatte,
und der sorgfältig nachmalenden Hand,
die den Sand ordnete, gegen alle Erfahrung.
So entstehen Strände, an denen wir ruhig
sitzen; oder auf die wir geworfen werden.

20. OKTOBER 1989

Vor meinem Fenster, dicht vor meinen Augen,
schnüffelt der Hund des Orion, der weiße Sirius,
durch die hungrigen Äste, kühl und betaut
in unendlicher Ferne. Verschwommen die Nähe,
die dünne Stimme des Radios: die Hauptstadt
rückt langsam nach Osten, in den Nacken der Welt.
Unbeschrieben wie sie sind verlieren die Träumer
erleichtert die Wette gegen sich selber:
das dünne Eis knistert und bricht
über den Worten. Eine Vergangenheit, ein Weg,
der Verzicht auf alle anderen Wege.
Dann kehren die Vögel zurück, die Wünsche
rücken zusammen und die Wolken.
Es wird hell in der Stube. Selbstvergessen,
angewidert vor dem Sortiment von Launen,
denke ich dem Ganzen hinterher:
zerstückelt zeigt die Welt sich im Gedicht.

NERO LEGTE SICH BLEI

Nero legte sich Blei
auf die Brust, seine Stimme
zu stärken. Jedes Wort
eine Narbe, eingebrannt
in das ungerechte Gedächtnis.
Andere leben von den Zinsen
des Schweigens, auch Fragen
ernähren den Mann.
Gegen nächtliches Irrereden
hilft ein Nagel,
aus einem Grabmal gerissen.
Ich kannte einen,
der ließ Insekten kriechen
über die leere Seite
seines Notizbuchs und las
in der dünnen Schattenschrift
sein Leben zu Ende.

NACHTS, UNTER BÄUMEN

FÜHRUNG

Was Sie hier sehen, ist der Geschichte abgetrotzt.
Alle Balken sind alt, auch die Türrahmen,
in denen früher die Toten hingen, drei Tage lang.
An diesem Tisch wurde Weltgeschichte geschrieben,
wie die Einkerbungen verraten: hier ein Galgen,
dort der Kopf des Königs. Wer die Frau sein soll,
die hier die Beine spreizt, können wir nur vermuten.
Kriege waren in Mode, weil es noch Schicksale gab,
die sich erfüllen mußten. Man hatte Ziele.
Aus seinem Mund ging ein scharfes Schwert, das heißt,
er konnte sich ausdrücken und wurde verstanden,
die Sprache war noch nicht erobert vom Zweifel,
sondern von Sicht geprägt, es existierte kein Archiv
der Leere. An diesem Tisch bezog der Mensch seine Identität
durch den Blick der anderen, auch auf Befehl.
Für die Angst gab es keinen Stuhl in diesem Raum,
sie nistete deshalb in den feinen Pinseln der Maler,
wie Sie an diesen Bildern sehen können: hier hat sie
überlebt, im Rausch der Farben. Die Bilder sind gereinigt
worden nach dem letzten Krieg. Obwohl uns die Tugenden
der Aufklärung wichtig bleiben, so sind sie doch nicht
absolut. Damals lernte man die Vögel einteilen in solche,
die man hört, und solche, die man sieht. Heute hören wir zu,
was uns die Stadt erzählt von Zeitstau und Verspätung.
Wenn Sie mir bitte folgen wollen, hier geht es zum
Ausgang.

DEUTSCHLANDLIEDCHEN

Stell dir vor, uns gehörte dies Haus,
das freundliche Knarren der Treppen
und die Mäuse hinter dem Holz.
Stell dir vor, am Tisch säßen mit uns
die Schatten derer, die einst hier
wohnten, und erzählten Gschichten.
Wir hörten zu. Trügen ihre Kleider,
am Kragen gewendet, in der Wolle
gefärbt. Und ein dicker Engel
der Geschichte schnitte Zwiebeln
und weinte für uns salzige Tränen.

Stell dir vor, wir bäten den Bach,
sein gekieseltes Bett zu verlassen,
damit der Fisch nicht über Land muß
auf dem Weg in unseren Topf.
Stell dir vor, wir schliefen nachts
in diesen Betten, und das Land
deckte uns zu mit seinen Träumen.

Stell dir vor, wir träumten, das Haus
verlassen zu müssen, und wüßten nicht
wohin.

DER PAPAGEI

Rede mir nicht von der Wahrheit,
bitte, nicht in diesem Haus
der Kunst. Frag die Fliege,
die auf Leben und Tod das Fenster
beackert, den Schmutz tanzen läßt
in schönen Figuren. Die Herrschaft
hat das Haus verlassen, frag nicht
wie, die Farbe ist noch feucht
auf der Leinwand, und im Computer
wartet ein kurzes Gedicht
auf seine letzte Zeile.
Nur die Gäste liegen noch faul
in den Sesseln, mundtot und müde
nach einem kurzen Gespräch.
Nichts kann mehr überschritten
werden, das ist die Wahrheit.
Rede mit den Steinen draußen,
die verträumt aus der Erde wachsen,
oder mit den Wolken, dem Regen.
Aber keine Anschauung, bitte,
nur heilige Zeichen. Ich bin
der Papagei des Hauses, mein Wortschatz
ist begrenzt wie der meiner Herrschaft,
deren Name mir entfallen ist.
Ich bin alt.
Und keine Fragen bitte! Denn gäbe es
eine Antwort, sie wäre in der Frage
verborgen. Mein Gefieder schreit
danach, beschrieben zu werden,
aber von draußen, durchs Fenster,
damit die Gäste nicht aufwachen.

DURCHSCHLAGPAPIER

Vielleicht, lese ich, war am Anfang das Kreuz
und über dem Kreuz eine fahle Sonne,
wie von Zauberschlag in den Himmel gesetzt.
Der Himmel ist überschrieben.
Ich erkenne das Duldergesicht, trotz der Spuren
von fremder Hand: zwei Schnecken als Augen,
das Skelett eines Fisches der Mund.
Ich lese verschwommen die unlesbare Liebe,
den Betrug der Sprache: ich weiß, du weißt,
selbst von Blinden leicht zu entziffern.

RATSCHLAG

Spare nicht mit der Farbe,
wenn du das Paradies malen willst
von seiner besten Seite. Zu wenig
davon glättet die Dinge, z. B.
das Meer sieht aus wie ein Begriff
vom Meer. Male nur eine Träne,
nur die Spiegelung deines Gesichts
in einem Wassertropfen,
dann hast du die Welle
und den Kiesel am Grund,
den Schiffbruch, das Paradies.
Zu wenig Farbe geht über
unsere Kräfte, und wir wollen ja,
daß sie unsere Sprache spricht
auf den Bildern. Wir haben immer
schon verstanden, was sich zeigt:
ein Haus am Meer
in einem heißen Sommer,
ganz weiß: als hätten wir in Schnee
gemalt.

BRIEF

Gestern abend ging ich – bitte
frag nicht: warum? – in die Kirche
im Dorf, hockte mich bibbernd
zwischen die alten Leute
in eine der engen Bänke
und bewegte die Lippen, als hätte ich
mitzureden. Es war ganz leicht.
Schon nach dem ersten Gebet – wir
beteten auch für Dich – wuchs mir
die Maske des Guten übers Gesicht.
Vorne pickte der alte Pfarrer,
ohne eine Lösung zu fordern,
wie ein schwarzer Vogel lustlos
im Evangelium, schien aber nichts
zu finden, uns zu verführen.
Kein Leitfaden, kein Trost.
Nach einer Stunde war alles vorbei.
Draußen lag ein unerwartet helles Licht
über dem See, und ein Wind kam auf,
der mich die Unterseite der Blätter
sehen ließ.

REPARATURWERKSTÄTTE

Ich wiederhole die Sätze der anderen,
die vor mir gesprochen haben, Beamte,
Direktoren, Angestellte, einfache Menschen.
Alle reden mehr oder weniger dasselbe:
mein Wagen stottert, ruckelt mächtig,
beschleunigt nicht, wenn ich es will.
Blindlings greife ich nach Worten
wie nach einem Werkzeug. Wenn etwas fehlt,
werde ich aufmerksam. Ich kann nichts
für meine Sprache, sie ist da und muß
gebraucht werden, sonst rostet sie ein.
Zu meiner Frau sage ich: das Essen ist gut.
Oder: ich liebe dich. Manchmal werfe ich
mich den Worten in die Arme, aber das ist
nicht gut fürs Geschäft. Gestern z.B.
war ein Dichter hier, uraltes Modell,
nicht zu verstehen. Seine Zündkerzen
waren verrußt, ganz einfach, aber er
konnte es nicht beschreiben, traurig.
Es ist ein Irrtum zu glauben, sagte er,
aber ich war schon längst unter der Haube.

NACHMITTAGS

Die Bücher im Fenster, dünn von der Sonne,
im Rücken das krachende Atmen der Seiten:
heben und senken, heben und senken …
Jedes trägt in sich, außer Romanen, Gedichten,
eine verborgene Sprache, ein paar Wörter
in einem trockenen Nest aus Papier, der Rest
ist verklumpte Grammatik.
Manchmal steigt ein Satz auf, den alle verstehen.
Zur Rede gestellt, befragt, bedrängt,
will ihn keiner gehört haben.

Ein Freund kommt zurück, bringt die Welt
ins Haus, den Berg, der brennend ins Meer fuhr,
die Vogelrufe, die Schneckenlinie des Zweifels.
Er berichtet von den Gegenden wie leere Klassenzimmer,
aus denen das Wissen vertrieben wurde.
Du übertreibst!
Aber schon schlägt er eine neue Seite auf,
zeigt auf ein Wasserzeichen, das Labyrinth
eines Fingers aus alter Zeit, zwei Daumen breit
vom Original entfernt.

Salze wuchern auf den Seiten, bilden Bäume,
auf deren dürren Zweigen Lügen wachsen.
Erwarte nichts. Zähle die Buchstaben, die Silben,
bis sich ein Wirt ergibt, dem du vertrauen kannst.
Es bringt dich zurück in den Satz.

GEDENKBLATT FÜR GÜNTER EICH

Im Garten stehen zwei Schuhe,
ein ungleiches Paar, außer Atem
nach einer langen Reise.
Verlebt und verwegen sehen sie aus
im taunassen Gras der Frühe.
Der eine knarrt in Prosa,
der andre in holprigen Versen.
Wir erfanden uns Wege,
die keines Menschen Füße je
berührt … Etwas geschwollen,
wenig glaubhaft, und überhaupt:
ein guter Schuh verrät den Weg
nicht, den er gekommen,
ein guter Schuh schweigt.
Ich könnte sie wegschmeißen,
lasse sie stehen. Am Morgen
sind sie auf und davon.

P.S.

für Marianne und Peter

Gestern gab es Apfelkompott von Äpfeln aus Tutzing,
die wir gleichsam von Geburt an kannten:
schon die Blüte hatten wir bewundert, ihren hellen
Schrei im Frühling, später die grünen Bällchen
und das Weißwerden des Grases nach dem Sturm.
Wir haben beobachtet, wie die Äpfel größer wurden
und sich mit Flecken überzogen, aber immer grün blieben,
grün-schwarze Äpfel. Schon im Sommer haben wir
daran gedacht, wie sie wohl im Herbst schmecken würden,
und als die ersten Äpfel im Gras lagen, Grün in Grün,
haben wir sie für die Hunde durch den Garten geworfen,
für Billie und Ella. Seiten vielen Jahren schon
verlassen wir uns auf die Äpfel im Tutzinger Garten.
Während die Welt (was immer das ist) uns nötigt,
die Relativität alles Wissens vorauszusetzen,
und wir nur noch verstehen, weil wir nichts mehr
durchschauen, ist die Lektion des Apfelbaums einfach:
altmodisch wird sie Jahr für Jahr wiederholt,
unabhängig davon, was Menschen voneinander halten,
mit einer Gewißheit, von der Vernunft nur träumen kann.
Kurz nach dem Frost, der Krieg war nach Westen gezogen,
haben wir die Äpfel gepflückt, die nun schon alt
aussahen, krank und hinfällig, wie es sich gehört.
Sie schmeckten besonders gut, etwas säuerlich,
so daß man nach dem ersten Bissen einhalten mußte.
Und gestern nun gab es den Rest als Kompott.
Beim Essen unterhielten wir uns lange darüber,
daß wir immer eine Realität voraussetzen müssen,
auf die wir dann reagieren können, so oder so.
Richtig glücklich waren wir nicht.

BRIEF AN EIN KIND
für Simon

Vielen Dank für Deinen Brief.
Der Umschlag, das frische Grün, hat mir gefallen,
ich will ihn aufheben, obwohl ich mich trennen will
von den Sachen. Wenn die Wohnung voll ist, muß ich sterben.
Deinen Umschlag habe ich an die Lampe geheftet,
jetzt ist es dunkler, das Papier nicht mehr weiß,
und Deine Schrift leuchtet: jetzt kann ich nie mehr
meinen Namen vergessen, meine Anschrift. Es gibt zu viel
von allem, wir müssen lernen, wegzuwerfen. Aber was?
Wenn ich morgens an der Mülltonne vorbeigehe,
kommen mir die Tränen. Gestern lag ein Mantel
unter Kaffeesatz und Kartoffelschalen, ein Ärmel hing
über den Rand des Containers, an dem ein Knopf fehlte.
Ein richtiger Mantel, wie ihn Menschen tragen.
Alles wird Geschichte, Müll, wenn ein Knopf fehlt,
ein lächerlicher Knopf aus Plastik.
Dieser Tage ist die große Sowjetunion
zerfallen, kein Mensch weiß, wie die Teile heißen,
aber jedes Teil hat einen Namen. Schöne Namen,
bei denen der Sprecher im Fernsehen stottert, der Mann
mit dem runden Gesicht. Alle Menschen sind jetzt Brüder,
sonst bleibt alles beim alten. Zuviel jetzt
in diesem Brief, wenig *gestern und morgen*, alles ist
zusammengerafft in diesem *jetzt*, auf den Punkt gebracht,
der etwas abschließt. Ob ich Dir einen Löwen bieten kann,
ist ungewiß. (Löwe wird übrigens mit *w* geschrieben,
mit einem Gruß an Deine Lehrerin.) Der Löwe jedenfalls,
der hier im Hause wohnt, sucht eine andere Wohnung.
Manchmal bringt er mir, mit triefendem Maul, die Post,
dann ist der Absender nicht mehr zu entziffern.
Ich schreibe sowieso nur noch Dir. Komm mich bald
besuchen, denn wenn Du erst groß bist, dann bin ich schon
tot.

BRIEF AN DAN PAGIS

Der Feind, lieber Freund, ist verschwunden.
Er hinterließ einen Zettel, braunes Papier:
du darfst dich um keinen Preis erinnern.
Manchmal, wenn ich auf dem Stuhl sitze,
auf dem Sie saßen, und die helle Landkarte
der Wolken einen wurmstichigen Schatten
auf der Straße auslegt, sehe ich das Pferd
des Totengräbers und erinnere mich an die Zeit,
da wir unsere Worte tauschten: Mein Name
ist Adam, dies ist Abel, mein guter Sohn,
stören Sie sich nicht an seinem Betragen.
Wir haben eine Karte gelöst bis ans Ende
der Welt, dürfen aber unterbrechen, so oft
wir wollen. Es wird immer einen Garten geben,
ein Haus, ein Kind, das vom Seewind träumt,
vom Feuer auf den Feldern. Es ist nicht gut,
zu lange zu sitzen. In dem Haus dort
haben wir früher gewohnt, es war ein Stall
für die Ziegen. Damals gab es noch viele Götter.
Und viele Zungen drängten sich verzweifelt
um wenige Wörter. Es gab kein Ende.
Kaum Verwaltung. Mein Vater, ein kluger Mann,
war beschäftigt mit der Lektüre der Symptome,
weil er die Krankheit abschaffen wollte, der Narr.
Seit seinem Tod sind wir unterwegs,
begleitet von Stimme und Schrift, unseren Schatten.
Dies, lieber Dan Pagis, wollten wir übersetzen,
Wort für Wort zur anderen Sprache bringen.
Bin ich das, der hier sitzt auf Ihrem Stuhl?

RÜCKKEHR IN EIN LEERES HAUS

Du hast vergessen, die Blumen zu gießen,
und im Aschenbecher liegt das trockene Gehäuse
eines Apfels, eine traurige braune Ruine
in einem Aschenfeld. Und überall Haare,
als wäre ein Tier hier verreckt. Im Fenster
Fliegen, die Beine nach oben, und eine Spinne,
die sich träge bewegt unter meiner Berührung.
Es ist nichts mehr zu ändern, alles ist staubig.
Kein Bild. Die Leiche im Ötztal, viertausend
Jahre alt, ein Bild des Menschen, hatte noch Haare,
als man sie fand unter dem Eis, und ein Lächeln
auf den Lippen, wahrscheinlich das erste
bekannte Lächeln in der kurzen Geschichte
der Menschheit, von dem sich alles herleitet
in der Kunst, ein Mensch zu sein. Irgendwann
hat es sich geteilt, wie die Wolke, die sich jetzt
vor dem Fenster teilt, keine abrupte Trennung,
sondern ein sanftes Lösen, ein flockiger Abschied,
mit dem Versprechen, einen winzigen Teil
des anderen mit sich zu führen für immer.
Ein Teil dieses Lächelns hat sich
mit dem Menschen verbündet, wenn er, unsicher,
über eine Schwelle stolpert, der andere ist
zu einem gewaltigen Lachen geworden,
das in kein Gesicht mehr paßt. Seither verbirgt
sich in jedem Gelächter ein Lächeln – und
umgekehrt, auch jetzt in diesem leeren Haus.
Alles kommt wieder zum Vorschein, ins Licht,
da der Schnee zu schmelzen beginnt, Zahn
um Zahn. Selbst die paar armseligen Wörter,
die uns, ohne Mühe, geblieben sind und die wir
für den Frühling versteckt haben, um einen Reim
zu finden auf Wiesen und Schafe und die Feier
des Lichts, werden sichtbar, aufgeweicht wie
Hundekot und einen matten Kranz um sich bildend,
aus dem sie sich schüchtern erheben: Anmutung,
Wiederkehr. Alles ist vorhanden, alles auch
der Abschied, das Ende, nur sieht alles anders
aus, wenn plötzlich einer die Decke wegzieht
von Abraum und Traum, und ein Lächeln befreit,
das auffliegt wie ein im Schlaf erschreckter Vogel.

Der Turm hob einen weißen Schleier an …
Die Erde, unheilbar krank, schwitzt ihre Toten aus
und hindert die Zukunft daran, Zukunft zu werden.
Geschirr in der Spüle. Der Kaffeesatz, eingetrocknet,
erzählt Geschichten zu meinen Gunsten, mit Anfang
und Ende, als hätte ich alles hinter mir.
Kein Schlaf zwischen den Zeilen, kein Ausruhn,
kein Tod, der uns tötet mit scharfen Augen.
Ich muß mich setzen, schwindlig ist mir
vor lauter Anruf, der hier aus der Stille dröhnt,
der Stille der Stille, dem Nabel der Sprache
unter dem Schnee. Vor dem Haus werden die Dinge
sichtbar, die Steine, die Frane, das braune Gras,
dazwischen die alten vergessenen Wege, die lange
vor der Straße die Richtung wiesen, der getretene
Pfad. Und dahinter der Wald, der mit Mühe
die hüpfenden Schatten der Rehe verbirgt,
bevor sie das Dunkel verschluckt. Und keine
Spur, also alles in Ordnung in diesem leeren
Haus. Auch den Computer hast du, selbstvergessen,
nicht abgestellt, ich sehe sein starres grünes
Auge, das andere Licht. Jetzt kennt er die Musik
auswendig, jeden Tom kann er simulieren
mit seinem unfehlbaren Gedächtnis. Alles ist
vorhanden. Alles geht mühelos auf einen Chip
von der Größe eines Daumennagels, Wort und Ton,
die ganze Geschichte, und wenn das Auge brennt,
ist alles mit uns, alles ist gleichzeitig,
auch ohne uns. Alles geht ohne uns, alles,
keiner sucht uns mehr. Jedes zarte Lächeln
und jedes Gelächter aus unvordenklichen Zeiten
hat Zutritt zu meiner Gegenwart. Alles läßt uns
teilnehmen, an allem nehmen wir teil.
Das tuschelnde Gewebe der Spuren, aus dem Bewußtsein
sich bildet, Geschichte und eine hauchdünne
Gegenwart, ist konzentriert in einem Punkt,
dem Punkt der unumkehrbaren Schönheit,
der jetzt langsam verlöscht. Wie lange war ich
nicht in diesem Haus?
Ich gehe von Foto zu Foto, lauter Fremde.
Einer war Philosoph, ich erkenne ihn wieder,
er hat den Tod in den Augen, der ihn ein Leben lang
liebte. Sie alle hängen hier, damit sie vergessen

werden. Da ist der Idiot, der Idiot der Familie,
der Zerstörer der Bücher, von dem die Familie
nicht wußte, ob er vom Wahnsinn befallen war
oder nur die Sprache des Wahnsinns beherrschte,
sein liebes zerknautschtes Gesicht, das er
auf die Erde preßte, um die Maulwürfe zu hören
bei der Arbeit. Die Menschen werden trauriger,
je länger sie hier hängen hinter Spinnweben
und Glas. Wie plötzlich alt gewordene Kinder
sehen sie aus, Kinder ohne Zukunft. Und dann
die Zeitzeugen, die bedruckte Natur. Die Geschichte
soll zu Ende sein, heißt es, mehr sei nicht
zu erwarten. Wir müssen leben von dem, was wir
haben und sind, ein Zuwachs ist nicht in Sicht,
keine Fortsetzung der Träume. Und keine Kunst.
Das also soll alles gewesen sein. vom Inzestverbot
bis zur freien Marktwirtschaft ein glatter
Durchmarsch. Die Röcke mal kürzer, mal länger,
irgendwann die Erfindung der Zentralperspektive,
die Zwölftonreihe, das drahtlose Telefon.
Selbstverständlich mußte einmal der Kopf des Königs
rollen, irgendwann war es Zeit für das freie
und allgemeine Wahlrecht. Wir erinnern uns noch
an den kreisenden Finger im Sand, an Kreide,
Bleistift, Schreibmaschine, die Historiker werden
herausfinden, ob Mörike mit der rechten Hands
schrieb oder mit der linken. Am Ende der Geschichte
wird die Geschichte siegen, die Geschichte des
Taschentuchs, mit dem die Tränen für immer aus dem
Gesicht der Erde gewischt wurden. Und alles nur
in unserem Kopf, in dem ein paar Drähte besser oder
anders vernetzt sind als bei den Hunden.
Ich beneide die Hunde. Ich möchte jedes Pferd
umarmen. Ich schaue jedem Vogel nach, jeder Krähe.
Jetzt also sollen wir Abschied nehmen von diesem
leeren Haus, von den erhabenen Blicken,
den herrischen Gesten, dem demütigen Wort,
der unmöglichen Gegenwart. Einmal aus der Hocke
aufgestemmt und ein paar Meter aufrecht
geradeaus gegangen, die Götter erfunden und schnell
wieder vergessen, und nun schon alles vorbei.
Eine durchsichtige Schleifspur läuft durch
das Haus, übers Papier, wie von Schnecken.

Und doch … Ich komme zu keinem Schluß, keinem
Anfang. Wenig Post. Einer will Geld, ein anderer
schickt Gedichte. Eines beschreibt feinfühlig
ein leeres Haus, in dem man von Zimmer zu Zimmer
gehen kann, ohne Hindernis, Wand oder Tür.
Das Haus ist leer. Ein schönes Gedicht
in freien Versen, so nutzlos und so entsetzlich
wahr.

AM TAG DANACH

Eigentlich wollte ich heute, am Montag,
ein kleines Liebesgedicht schreiben,
ein unscheinbares Poem über ein Paar,
das ich gestern in einer Kneipe ("Kosta")
beobachtet hatte. Ich wollte nicht
"Gottes Sprache nachahmen", wie Dante,
oder zur Ironie greifen, sondern einfach
das Geflecht aus Macht, Begehren und Wissen,
wie es sich mir, dem nervösen Beobachter,
darstellte, beschreiben: in Satzfetzen,
Blicken, Haltungen, an der Art, wie der Mann
neuen Wein bestellte, die Frau rauchte.
Es sollte ein Liebesgedicht werden,
das mit keinem Wort an die in Auflösung
begriffene Kultur erinnern sollte,
die mich den ganzen Tag beschäftigt,
weil sie nicht aufzuhalten ist.
Nach der Natur der Poesie zu fragen,
fordert zur Reflexion über den Stand
unserer Existenz heraus. Wer ihre Fehler,
die Fehler der Poesie, nicht erforscht,
wird sie wiederholen, da hilft auch nicht
die Anrufung der Freiheit, die sich
angeblich im Gedicht realisiert, sogar noch
im Bruch seiner Zeilen. Ich stellte mir vor:
die einfältige Utopie einer geglückten
Berührung, die nicht an Tod, Zerstörung,
Katastrophen denkt. Aber die Worte
weigerten sich, ihre Wahrheit preiszugeben,
als wüßten sie nicht, wie Anschauung,
Wissen, in Sprache übersetzt wird.
Vielleicht ist das der Grund, warum
Liebesgedichte heute so kurz ausfallen,
warum ihre Ergebnisse, wenn diese Sprache
erlaubt ist, so vorhersehbar sind.

IM GESPRÄCH

Du weißt: ich bin nur ein Gast hier
in diesem Haus, einer, der den Schatten
aufsucht unter den großen Bäumen,
das flüchtige Bündnis am Abend.
Ich bin das Auge, während der Wind
in der Hecke liest und dem Bach,
der sich meerwärts müht, eine Fratze
auf den Rücken malt, zum Schutz
gegen die Nacht, die noch wartet.
Zwischen Weggang und Wiederkehr
glitzert zweideutig das Salz
in der fallenden Sonne.
Du weißt, an wen ich mich wende,
an das Gesicht, das mich erblickt,
ohne mich zu erkennen. Der Tag
ist um, die Wächter steigen weiß
aus dem Gras und halten Gericht,
doch immer so, daß sie es sich
mit Gott nicht verderben.

FORTSETZUNG FOLGT

Im Hause stehen noch die Mausefallen
vom letzten Mieter und in den Ecken
Schälchen, voll mit rotem Gift,
das den Fliegen schmecken soll,
bevor sie sterben. Schwarze Käfer
liegen auf dem Rücken, als hätten sie
versucht, die Luft zu treten.
Nur die Spinnen scheinen sich
hier wohlzufühlen, die mit zarten Beinchen
den Roman erzählen, dessen Ende
wir nicht kennen. Am Anfang, heißt es,
stand ein Mord, der einen roten Faden
hinterließ auf allen Mauern dieses Hauses.
Dann kam die Zeit des Opfers, dann:
der Krieg. Jetzt wohnen wir hier.
Warten auf den Wind, der all die Wörter
wieder heimholt aus dem leeren Himmel.

176

DAS BETT

für Ariane

Als du weggegangen warst,
habe ich dein Bett abgezogen.
Die Matratze sah aus
wie ein abgerissener Sträfling.
Wenn ich jetzt das Licht lösche,
bin ich mir nicht mehr sicher,
auf welcher Seite ich liege.
Mit einem Bein im Gefängnis,
mit dem anderen in der Freiheit,
an Schlaf ist nicht zu denken.

BLICK IN DEN GARTEN

Könnte ich doch die flatternden Wimpern
des Lorbeers, die im Sturm auffliegen
und sich erst wieder senken, wenn die Schatten
ihren Schatten nehmen vom dunklen Grün,
mit Worten beschreiben, die ihnen gemäß sind.
Nicht die Schönheit ist ein Privileg dessen,
der hinter dem Fenster steht und starrt
auf die gesäumten Wege, den Brunnen,
dem die Steine davonlaufen, und die Kräuter,
nach Klassen geordnet wie in der Schule,
sondern die Worte sind es, die ungeduldig
in einem hocken wie in einer atmenden Arche
und auf das Ende des Regens warten.
Manche verlassen den Mund zu früh
und fliegen erschrocken davon, andere
bleiben in der ihnen zugewiesenen Hülle.
Wir wählen unsere Sprache, nicht umgekehrt,
und auch das lautlose Prahlen der Augen
sucht sich die richtigen Worte, wenn die Zeit
dafür kommt. Aber manchmal, wenn man still
hinter dem Fenster steht und dem Lorbeer
zusieht, wie er kokett sich dem Wind überläßt,
fängt es von selbst an und sagt:
flatternde Wimpern.

WIND

Eine einfache, allgemeine Antwort,
die das Sandkorn wie die Sterne, den Gott
wie den Wurm umfaßt. Ein Werkzeug, eine Zange:
nur in der Welt sind die Instrumente zu finden,
an denen die Welt sich messen läßt. Ich stehe
am Fenster. Unten kläfft ein Hund einen Hund an,
überzieht ihn mit gurgelnden Lauten. Die Frau,
die ihn hält, studiert murmelnd die Preise
in der Auslage des Juweliers. Ich sehe
ihre sich bewegenden Lippen im Spiegel des Fensters:
ein Gebet soll ihr helfen. Lieber Gott ...
Man versuche, sich einen Gott vorzustellen
mit unendlicher Begabung. Der andere Hund
läßt sich zitternd beschimpfen. Warum läuft er
nicht weg? Er hat eine Erfahrung gemacht
und könnte sich trollen. Gott ist nur ein halber
Mensch, immer dieselben, identischen Antworten:
Erfahrung ist für ihn ein sinnloser Begriff.
Die Menschen gehen jetzt schneller, als würde
ein Wind ihnen Beine machen, eine unsichtbare Kraft.
Alles schwimmt vorüber, alles bleibt stehen,
schlägt den Kragen hoch gegen den beißenden Wind,
der die Sätze mitnimmt und verwandelt
in eine einfache, allgemeine Antwort.

REDE DES MALERS

Ich habe, wie so viele vor mir, der Schönheit
geopfert. Meine Hand war der Priester, ein Asket
der Farben. Sie vernarrte sich in dunkle Flächen
von hellgrau bis blauschwarz, Menschen und Dinge
ließ sie nicht zu. So entstand, Bild für Bild,
ein aschiges Haus für die Schönheit, die selber
abwesend blieb. Soll ich noch einmal beginnen?
Meine Arbeit ist getan. Jetzt schläft die Welt
in meiner Hand und zuckt bei schweren Träumen
mit den blinden Augen. Mein Bild ist fertig.
Ich werde nicht mehr malen.

REDE DES MUSEUMSWÄRTERS

Ich habe die Welt gesehen
im Bild. (Mich selbst sah ich
im salzweißen Auge des Hasen,
das um Unsterblichkeit bittet
in der Sekunde des Todes.)
Und hatt' an allen Toden teil.

REDE DES NARREN

Glauben Sie mir, ich verstehe die Sprache
der Vögel: die rollenden Pfiffe des Kleibers
und das nervöse Geplapper der Drosseln,
auch der wilde Kehrreim des Kauzes
und das metallische Prasseln des Zeisigs
sind mir nicht fremd. Wenn diese Vögel
schüchtern zuerst und zögernd,
am Morgen ihr Preislied beginnen,
durchsetzt von den rauhen Klagen der Elstern
und dem knarrenden Geschwätz der Krähen,
wenn Finken und Grasmücken, Ammern und Lerchen
ihren Gesang ein üben, verstehe ich jedes Wort.
Die Ärzte sind ratlos.
Sie hören nicht den Befehl des Bluthänflings,
mit dem er den Tag beendet, verstehen nicht
die schrillen Schreie der Mauersegler,
wenn sie den Sommer einrollen für die Reise
nach Süden. Für den, der hört, geben die Töne
sich Zeichen, Flötenruf und wirres Krakeel
ziehen sich an, bis ein Satz entsteht,
eine Erzählung mit Lockruf und Warnung,
die auffliegt im schwachen September,
eine bräunliche Spreu auf der Leinwand
des Himmels, die gut zu lesen ist im Winter.

REDE DES ÜBERSETZERS

für Friedhelm Kemp

Mehr als hundert Mal habe ich
den Mond übersetzt, den Freund
der Dichter, ohn ihn zu verraten.
Ich habe ihn kursiv zerfließen lassen
oder ihn halbfett ernährt,
wenn er am Abnehemen war.
Auch die Seufzer, als Teil der Sprache,
die ihn umkreist, habe ich
nach bestem Wissen übertragen
in die geschwätzige Zeit.
Das Ah! stand ihm besser als das Oh! –
statistich gesprochen.
*Alles is neu zu tun, alles
ist neu zu sagen,* war mein Motto.
Bezalt wurde ich nur für eine Silbe:
Mond.
Benutzen Sie eine Bezeichnung
für jeden Begriff, sagt der Direktor
der Sprachbank, das ist gut
für die Verständigung unter den Völkern.
Worte sind niemandes Eigentum
und kommen uns doch teuer zu stehen
in barer Münze. Der Wortbedarf steigt
mit dem nationalen Reichtum,
also sparen Sie, wo Sie können,
belassen Sie es einfach bei:
Mond.

REDE DES VERZWEIFELTEN

Keine Zeit mehr, das Versäumte nachzuholen,
die Wege zu schlecht, der Karren zu klein,
nur das, was in die Manteltasche paßte,
ist noch bei uns. Manchmal fragen wir uns,
was es ist: es fühlt sich kühl an und rund,
wie der versteinerte Kopf eines Tieres.
Da, wo wir jetzt leben, ist sowieso kein Platz
für Versäumtes. In unserer neuen Wohnung
hält sich die Gegenwart auf. Sie sitzt
mit am Tisch, wenn wir essen, nachts liegt sie
schwitzend in unserem Bett und träumt
den besseren Teil unserer Träume,
wenn wir zur Arbeit gehen, knistert sie leis
zwischen den Akten. Öffnen wir endlich
den Mund, um ihr unsere Meinung zu sagen,
spricht sie für uns von ihren Zielen.
Wenn wir sie nicht beobachten, schreibt
die Gegenwart mit unserem Stift Gedichte,
um sich am Wort zu halten. Für das Sonett
"Die Kälte ist die Zukunft" – "alle Geschichte
ist eine Geschichte der Temperatur" – .
erhielt sie den Großen Preis der Akademie.
Die Natur ist ästhetisch unvollkommen,
heißt es darin, sie verarmt, nimmt zu,
vermischt sich, wie sie will. Erst das Zerbrechen
der Steine erzeugt die Individualität der Steine,
richtig gereimt. Und wir, so schließt es,
sind der klumpige Sand am Grab der Identität.
Kein Wunder, daß wir mit Liebe des Versäumten
Gedenken.

BRIEF VOM 1. FEBRUAR 1995

Vielen Dank für den Anruf neulich.
Ich war so sprachlos, weil meine Schwester
gerade gestorben war und ein großer Teil
unserer gemeinsamen Jugend mit ihr.
Man merkt, wie wenig einem gehört,
und der Rest langt nicht für eine Geschichte
mit Anfang und Ende.
Außerdem gab es ein Wintergewitter,
in dem sich ihre freundlichen Worte verloren.
Der Wind zwang die Bäume zu Haltungen,
daß selbst die Vögel erschraken.
Man sah ihnen die Erleichterung an,
als sie wieder aufrecht stehen durften.
Und schließlich knackt es seit Tagen
in der Heizung, als wäre eine Erzählung
darin eingesperrt, die sich befreien will.
Ein eigentümlicher Dialekt, der nur
in diesem Haus gesprochen wird.
Ja, ich arbeite noch, und wahrscheinlich
werde ich bis zum Ende nicht unterbrechen.
Die Philosophen, las ich kürzlich,
wären schon zufrieden, wenn sie ein paar
neue Fragen fänden – ich dagegen bin gierig
nach Antworten. Das schwache Echo
einer einzigen kümmerlichen Antwort,
das mir ins Gesicht spränge und bliebe,
wäre genug.

IM FEBRUAR 1995

Dort, wo die Flüsse
schäumend ineinanderstürzen
und die Namen tauschen,
gibt es, bei hohem Pegel,
ein abgespaltnes, kleines Becken,
nicht der Rede wert:
Mitgift der Schmelze.
Ein stiller Ruheplatz
für Wasservögel,
die nicht zu wissen scheinen,
mit welchem Strom sie ziehen sollen
bis zum Meer.
Für mich, den Zweifler,
ist die Brücke da,
ein Ungeheuer aus Beton,
das die Natur
mit hohem Bogen überspannt.

NACHTS, UNTER BÄUMEN

Bäume, in loser Reihung
raumscheu verteilt
auf dem sich neigenden Hang.
Ein Stern schon abgekauft
dem mächtigen Schädel der Nacht,
ihn brachte das Käuzchen.
Die Worte bleiben dir treu,
während es in dich einströmt,
keins verrät sich und dich.
Erst am Ende der Nacht,
verbracht unter Bäumen,
klärt sich dein eignes Beginnen,
weil die Antwort verschont bleibt
vom Fragen.

AKTENNOTIZ

Nachts hörte ich wieder
die Schreie der Vögel,
und das Gras hörte mit.
Waffenstillstand, scharf
geladen mit einem Wort,
das bleibt. Fünfzig Jahre
hat uns Hitler ernährt,
jetzt sollen die anderen
essen, wir schauen zu
wie sie verrecken,
die Gabel im Hals.
Nachts höre ich wieder
die Schreie der Vögel,
das geflügelte Epos
der Angst.

ZUR ERINNERUNG AN CIORAN

Genug gelacht gegen die Schöpfung.
Jeder geknickte Halm ein Beweis,
jeder Tautropfen eine Träne,
jeder Brief ein Erschrecken.
Von Christus gar nicht zu reden,
der ihn liebte wie einen Bruder,
den es zu opfern gilt,
um die eigne Macht zu beweisen.
Der Fußtritt war das Wasserzeichen
seines Schreibens, ein Slapstick,
ständig wiederholt: jahrelang
beweinte er schlaflos die Schöpfung,
jetzt starb er friedlich im Schlaf.

ERZIEHUNG

Ich gehöre nicht zu denen,
die ihre Mutter begehrten oder
den störenden Vater töten wollten.
Der elterliche Verkehr, mein Gott,
mich trieben andere Phantasien
aus dem Haus. Auch die Lichtgarbe
des Kometen am nächtlichen Himmel
war für mich kein spermatischer Ausfluß.
Und der Regenbogen, den ich so liebe,
verband nicht Mann und Weib (oder Frau),
sondern Himmel und Erde.
Doch manchmal frage ich mich,
ob mein Ohr weiß, was es hört,
mein Auge weiß, was es sieht.
Wenn ich Maria sehe, wie sie dem Kinde
die Brust gibt, kann ich nicht glauben,
daß der zerredete Körper
der christlichen Kultur seine Seele
ausgehaucht hat. Und schließlich:
der melancholische Hund, mein Hund,
er darf nicht der unterwürfige Sohn sein!
Jeder muß sich etwas ausdenken,
das er für wahr hält: ausdrücklich oder
verschwiegen, aber am Ende zählt nur
die undurchdringliche Welt.

GERÜCHT 1995

Es geht ein Gespenst um
in Deutschland, klein
soll es sein und sprechen
in versehrten Worten
wie ein fremdes Kind.
Und einen Mantel
soll es tragen,
viel zu groß
für seinen greisen Körper.
Und geht in Stiefeln,
heißt es, hochgeschnürt,
die klicken einen Rhythmus
auf der Schädelnaht,
den wir nicht kennen sollen.
Kennt sich nicht aus.
Rupft den Kalender ab
mit schnellem Finger.
Kennt seinen Namen
nicht und lacht,
wenn es uns sieht,
wie wir es sehen.
Ist nicht von hier.

DIE KLEINEN VERSE

Die kleinen Verse, die keine Richtung kennen,
keine Tendenz, sie folgen selbstvergessen
einem Weg ins Dunkel und tauchen plötzlich
auf der Lichtung auf, verwandelt. Sie kennen
nicht den Appetit auf große Wörter, sie sagen
nicht, was Menschen tun und lassen sollen.
Und wenn von Gottes Tod die Rede ist,
vom Tod des Menschen, sind sie nicht zu hören.
Platon, Nietzsche, alle Dichter, die mit Feuer
das Feuer bekämpfen, daß im fiebrigen Prasseln
Klang werde, höherentwickelte Form, verachten
die kleinen Verse. Sie aber leben weiter,
im Lidschlag des Auges, das sich öffnet und
schließt.

AN ZBIGNIEW HERBERT

Weil ein träges und mageres Bächlein
im Frühjhar, in den Wochen der Schmelze,
oft ein größeres hervortreten läßt,
ein aufbrausendes Wasser, das die Ufer
mitnimmt bei raschem Durchgang,
starren jetzt viele, der Gegenwart müde,
auf den schwindenden Vorrat der Träume,
ob sich nicht etwas zeige am Grund:
eine andere Sprache unter der Sprache,
mit der sich erklären ließe, warum wir
erklären wollen, als sei nicht genug.
Nicht die Routine, die wir Leben nennen,
den untreuen Kopf, der alles vergißt,
damit wir am Morgen die Sonne erkennen
mit Ah! und Oh!
Die Welt sei nur Einbildung, sagen jetzt
viele nach einem ersten Blick ins Gehirn
und sind schon verloren im Virtuellen,
wo ein Baum nur noch aussieht wie einer.
Und an der Grenze?
Steht ein Spiegel, so groß wie die Welt,
der einen Baum zeigt, der keiner ist:
was Realität hieß in unserem Land
ist von der Illusion der Realität nicht
mehr zu trennen. Hat sich die Welt
verändert, seit der *Meder* kam – oder nur
das Wissen über die Welt, das sie
zum Verschwinden bringt in ihrer
Wiederholung? Bald, lieber Zbigniew,
werden wir alle Spiegel im Lande
verhängen und die Bilder zur Wand kehren,
damit das Bild, das uns zeigt,
den nicht aufhält, der am Ende
unvorstellbaren Welten entgegenwandert.

SCHRIFTSTELLERKONGREß
Lahti/Finnland

Einmal habe ich, heimlich, von meinem Fenster aus,
in der unerbittlichen Helle der Mittsommernacht,
den Dichtern zugehört, die auf dem fleckigen Rasen
vor dem Hotel die Schönheit besprachen, ihre
beleidigte Wahrheit. Dem kleinäugigen Russen,
der seinen Schatten unter dem Arm trug, wie nur
ein Russe, in der Mißgunst der kalkigen Frühe,
einen Schatten balancieren kann. Wenn uns im Schlaf
die Worte erreichen, anlegen zwischen zwei Atemzügen
in der sanften Dünung des Morgens, entsteht jene
Stimmung von Einheit und Unendlichkeit,
aus der Gedichte herauswachsen wie das dürre Gras
aus rissigem Asphalt. Einen traurigen Schweden,
der aussah wie der stumme Gott der Identität,
müde vom Spielen mit Wörtern. Nur ein Hauch noch,
eine Silbe, ein Echo in einer Folge von Spiegeln,
die keinen Anfang kennen und kein Ende.
Einer Portugiesin, eingehüllt in wehende Tücher,
die vom Flattern des Habichtweibchens sprach
bei seiner ersten Deckung: so empfangen die Wörter
unseren Sinn, wie der Zweig im Frühling,
wenn der Saft der Erde in ihn dringt. Schließlich
einem Dichter aus Polen, nur der Wahrheit treu,
die es nicht gibt in den Sätzen, einem Mann
mit dunklen Augen, verirrt in seiner Melancholie.
Er zeigte den andern eine Münze, um die Lage
der Poesie zu erläutern: weder Kopf noch Zahl
waren zu sehen auf dem abgegriffenen Rund.
Eine Totenmesse für die leere Stelle zwischen
Geist und Natur unter einem blaugrauen Himmel.
Ich selbst hatte, den Kopf hinterm Vorhang verborgen,
dies und das auf der Zunge über den Anspruch
der Wahrheit der poetischen Rede, blieb aber stumm,
wärmte die aufkommenden Schreie in meinem Mund,
die ein Teil der Wahrheit waren, deren Geschichte
als blutiger Irrtum bekannt ist. Ein machtloser Teil,
geplündert, entheiligt, unfähig, das Zerrissene
zu nähen. Aber ich konnte nicht sprechen, sah nur
im Spiegel des Fensters mein Gesicht, verschwommen
wie geschmolzenes Pech. Später, die Mitternacht

war längst vorüber, gesellte sich ein schlafloser
französischer Dichter zu den andern. Er hatte
Kiesel gesammelt unten am See, in der Helle der Nacht,
verfolgt von den krächzenden Schreien der Möwen,
die zeigte er vor: Wir stehen außerhalb der Literatur,
wenn wir über sie reden, sagte er, jedes Wort war
deutlich zu hören, wir verdoppeln sie nur, ohne sie
selbst zu berühren, ihren harten, unzerstörbaren Kern.
Laßt uns Gäste sein, ungebeten, aber willkommene,
zufällige Gäste, die an der Tafel Platz nehmen
und wieder verschwinden, ohne daß sie jemand vermißt.
Der Pole schwieg. Der Russe entließ seinen Schatten
und hüpfte ihm nach. Die Portugiesin, wie eine Mumie
verhüllt, dachte wohl an die Wörter, welche die Schönheit
des Körpers feiern, unbeeindruckt vom Tod. Der Schwede
ging lächelnd von dannen wie einer, der die Schwäche
dessen kennt, was er tut. Ich selbst blieb stehen
hinter dem Fenster und schaute dem Wind zu,
der in dem hellen Grün der Birken Ruhe fand.

DER FRIEDHOF

Gleich beim Eingang, neben dem Komposthaufen,
wo die Gladiolen ihr süßliches Rot aushauchen,
liegt ein Dichter, den ich gut kannte. Er hatte
ein paar Wörter aus dem Krieg heimgebracht
(im Schuh versteckt), die er so lange wendete,
bis sie ein Buch ergaben: vierundsechzig Seiten
und ein Eintrag im Brockhaus, der nach seinem Tod
wieder verschwand. Gerühmt wurde seine Trauer,
seine Bildhaftigkeit und seine Herkunft von Loerke
(dem er nie begegnet war). Auch die falschen Reime
auf ein falsches Leben sind ihm zu verdanken.
(Einen Künder nannte ihn Benn, aber der Brief
ist verlorengegangen, so gibt's keinen Täter
hinter der Tat.) Er hatte nie Geld, aber Musen,
die sein Geschirr spülten und die Gedichte verschickten,
wenn er müde und traurig auf dem Sofa lag.
Er spürte den starren Blick, der aus der Zukunft
auf ihn fiel und seine Wörter bleichte.
In der Reihe dahinter ruht einer, der in den sechziger Jahren
die Poesie konkret werden ließ: auch ein Gott ist
nur ein Wort, da jubelten die Atheisten.
Lange Wortketten, lose übers Blatt gestreut,
und er das letzte Glied, das nicht mehr greift:
ein Leckerbissen für Theoretiker, die seine Texte
mit Sand verglichen, mit Wüste, warum auch immer.
Wenn man ihn traf, kam er gerade von einem Kongreß,
oder aber erfuhr zu einem Symposion nach Celle,
immer zweiter Klasse und mit Wörterbüchern bepackt,
die er mit spitzen Fingern umgrub auf der Suche
nach seltenen Schätzen: Darhöhung, für Brandopfer,
du verstehst nicht, daß du verstehen mußt.
Er trank sich zu Tode. Sein Name, kleingeschrieben,
hat bereits einige Buchstaben verloren,
das hätte ihn vermutlich gefreut. (In São Paulo
ist kürzlich eine Anthologie erschienen, in der er
als wirklicher Revolutionär gefeiert wird.)
Seine Frau, konventioneller begabt, schrieb auch
Gedichte. In einem verglich sie die Langsamkeit
eines Menschen mit dem Lidschlag der Eule. Mein Gott,
was mußte sie sich von der Kritik sagen lassen.
Sie hätte ihre Wörter gestohlen, war noch das mindeste.

Aber wem gehören die Wörter? Wahrscheinlich lebt sie
noch und wischt mit gichtigen Fingern das Blut
vom Marmor – An der Mauer zur Straße, vom Lärm
überspült, den er so oft besang, liegt das Grab
des einzigen politischen Dichters der Stadt.
Er war sehr berühmt, man lernte ihn auswendig,
jedes Gedicht ein zärtlicher Faustschlag, kurz,
trocken und schön: Die Welt zeigt ihr braunes Gebiß.
Zwei Jahre war er mein Nachbar, dann zog er aufs Land
oder ließ sich ziehen von einer Frau, die heute
seine Unterschrift fälscht, um die Miete zu zahlen.
Ein Grab kann ich nicht finden. Der Wächter schüttelt
den Kopf. Ein Dichter? Hier? Keine Ahnung, ob
hier auch Dichter liegen, man sieht's ja den Gräbern
nicht an. Er soll sich erhängt haben. Von einem Unfall
sprach die Familie, die es sich leisten konnte,
seine Gedichtbände aufzukaufen und zu vernichten.
Ich war mit ihm in Rom, in den achtziger Jahren,
da schrieb er lange Poeme über Kaiser, Päpste
und Katzen in einer Sprache, die so fremd war
und funkelnd, daß keiner sie verstand. Heute rühmen
sich einige Kenner, sein Talent schon immer erkannt
zu haben, sie loben den hohen Ton, der Haß, Schönheit
und Trauer im alten Gesetz vereinte, daß eure Augen
sich klären. Ich höre noch sein Lachen, wenn er
über die Kritiker sprach, die in der Kunst des Gedichts
eine Entwicklung sahen, als käme es nicht nur darauf an,
den Vogelschwarm zu sehen, der vom Hauptbahnhof
in Richtung Colosseum flog, wo er wohnte. Vogelflug,
sich selbst löschende Schrift … Sein Grab war nicht
zu finden. Was war noch zu tun? Er hatte mir ein Gedicht
geschenkt, eine Vorschrift des Todes, gereimt,
geschrieben um Dunkeln, im Licht der Augen einer Katze,
das fiel mir jetzt ein. Vor dem Friedhof stand
eine hell leuchtende Telefonzelle, ich ging hinein,
nahm den Hörer von der Gabel und sprach mich langsam
aus.

DER LETZTE TAG DES JAHRES

Als wollte der Himmel der Erde eine Entschädigung abstatten,
hat der Regen heute die Bilder aus den Rahmen gewaschen,
die jetzt einen hellen Fleck umgrenzen auf den streifigen Wänden.
Die Welt, die kommen wird! Nur die Erinnerungen behalten
ihre trübe Farbe. Das Jahr verklumpt in seinen letzten Stunden.
Sage keiner, es läge noch viel zwischen Becher und Lippe,
wenn den Fortschritt noch eine Handbreit vom Rundgang trennt,
denn im Grunde, und diese Lektion mußten wir nicht lernen,
fängt mit jedem Tag ein neues Jahr an: das Jahr des Krieges.
Und ist keine Allegorie wie der sich lümmelnde Engel
mit der Gasmaske in den lächelnden Galaxien. Jetzt ist
die Posaune zu hören, die den dritten Teil der Sonne
verfinstert, ohne daß jemand es bemerkt, und der Rest
verglüht wie der grüne Punkt im TV nach den Nachrichten,
den letzten des Jahres. Die Gnade, die auch ihre Feinde liebt,
hat sich im Datum geirrt, ihr falscher Zungenschlag hat sie
hinübergestottert ins neue Jahr, als der Eroberer längst
zurückerobert war: in Fesseln war er zu sehen, wie sie ihn,
gut sichtbar, über den ockerfarbenen Marktplatz der Bilder
schleiften in seiner eigenen Blutspur. Auf den Augen des Toten
wachsen Landschaften, eine erhabene Ruine, das gereimte Tuscheln
der Palmen, ein Brummen ohne Worte, schattiert und schraffiert,
eingefangen von unserem besten Maler, der sich scheu versteckt
hinter seiner Kamera. Ça va mal, très mal, so der Demiurg,
der das Unleserliche noch einmal buchstabiert, in Reinschrift:
Nachrufe, für das Auge bestimmt. Noch eine Stunde. Zeit wird's,
daß sich die Feinde zeigen. Das Leben ist von der Erde
verschwunden und nur noch in den Tiefen des Oceans zu finden.
War es Kant, der unsere Fortdauer auf dem Jupiter voraussah?
Schicksal ist jedenfalls kein Thema mehr, zu tief stehen wir
in der Kreide, und die treibenden Eismassen dehnen sich weit
und immer weiter aus. Wer weiß, vielleicht ist auch dieser
besondere Augenblick durch eine Anregung von oben
in die Welt gekommen, diese Sekunde, da man endgültig abkippt
ins Stillschweigen. Ich sehe dem Regen zu und der vom Wind
mißhandelten Hecke und der Nacht, die mit schwerer Zunge
mit den Aufräumarbeiten beginnt, damit das neue Jahr sich
zeigen kann von seiner alten Seite.

KURZ VOR DEM GEWITTER

WO ICH GEBOREN WURDE

1

Mein Großvater konnte über hundert Vögel
an ihren Stimmen erkennen, nicht gerechnet
die Dialekte, die in den Hecken gesprochen wurden,
dunklen Schulen hinter dem Hof,
wo die Braunkehlchen Aufsicht hatten.
Mein Großvater war Spezialist für Kartoffeln.
Mit den Händen grub er sie aus, zerbrach sie
mit den Daumen, die weiß wurden,
und ließ mich an der Bruchstelle lecken.
Mehlig, gut für Schweine und Menschen.
Auch nach der Enteignung wollte er unbedingt
an Gott glauben, weshalb ich die Kartoffeln
ausbuddeln mußte aus seinem ehemaligen Acker.
Wie auf holländischen Bildern zogen
schwere Wolken über den sächsischen Himmel,
sie kamen aus Rußland und Polen
und fuhren nach Westen, ihre Fracht wurde leichter,
durchsichtiger und feiner, bis sie in Frankreich
als Seide verkauft wurde. Im Westen, sagte er,
finden Verwandlungen statt, wir werden verwandelt.
Im Dorf fehlten einige seiner Freunde.
Die mußten in Rußland die Wolken beladen.

2

Meine Großmutter benutzte die Brennschere,
um ihre dünnen Haare zu wellen. Man muß
dem Herrgott ordentlich frisiert gegenübertreten.
Der kam meistens nachts, wenn ich schon
schlafen sollte, setzte sich auf den Bettrand
und unterhielt sich mit ihr auf sächsisch.
Beide flüsterten, als hätten sie ein Geheimnis.
Manchmal waren sie freundlich zueinander,
dann wieder zankte sie mit ihm wie
mit dem Großvater, wenn er sein Glasauge
neben den Teller legte. Wenn man es falsch herum
einsetzt, kann man nach innen sehen,
in den Kopf hinein, wo die Gedanken leben,
sagte er und stopfte seine Pfeife mit Eigenbau,
der neben dem Tisch an der Wand hing, labbrige Blätter,
von einem Faden durchzogen. Die Ärmel der Joppe

des Großvaters waren von Brandlöchern genarbt.
Wie deine Lunge, sagte die Großmutter, beides
aus braunem Stoff. So vergingen die Tage.
Abends gab es Kartoffeln mit Sauce oder ohne.
Wenn auf dem Hof geschlachtet wurde, fand ich
Wellfleisch auf meinem Teller, aber ich durfte nicht
fragen, wie es zu uns gefunden hatte.
Wellfleisch kann fliegen, damit war alles gesagt.
Ich stellte mir Gott als einen Menschen vor,
der alles mit sich machen ließ.

3

Mein Großvater las nicht mehr. Alle Bücher stehen
in meinem Kopf, sagte er, aber ganz durcheinander.
Dafür erzählte er gerne, am liebsten vom König,
der sich angeblich für ihn interessiert hatte.
Auf der Jagd sollte er ihm einen Hasen
vor die Flinte treiben, aber der Großvater hatte
das Tier unter seinem Mantel versteckt.
Ich kann noch heute das Hasenherz schlagen hören,
rief er und faßte sich an der Stelle, wo seine Uhr
hing. Hasen haben ein schlechtes Herz,
damit kann man keinen Staat machen. Vom Staat
war nicht viel zu erwarten. Wenn die Großmutter
nicht im Zimmer war, hörten wir Radio, messerscharfe
Stimmen, die den Rauch seiner Pfeife zittern ließen.
Saubande sagte mein Großvater, der sonst nie
fluchte. In der Nähe von Beromünster war die Musik
zu Hause, da fahren wir eines Tages hin, sagte er,
und hören Bach und Tschaikowsky. Dann schlief er ein.
Das Lid über seinem Glasauge war nie ganz geschlossen.

4

Als ich mein Dorf kürzlich besuchte,
fiel mir alles wieder ein, nur ungeordnet:
der Kunsthonig und der schwarze Sirup, der sämig
durch die Löcher im Brot tropfte, die fauchenden Feuer
über Meuselwitz, die kyrillischen Gewehre im Steinbruch
von Keyna, der Kohlenstaub, Warmbier, der ängstliche Gott,
der schnatternde Alarmruf des Wiedehopfs,
die puckernden Flüsse auf dem Handrücken des Großvaters,

der blaue Teppich unter den Pflaumenbäumen,
die Eselsohren in der Bibel, die fromme Armut,
das Glück. Auch die Toten redeten mit, von fern her
angereist in altmodischen Kleidern, die Frauen
mit Haarnetzen, die Männer in gewendeter Uniform,
mit Schußlöchern auf der eingefallenen Brust.
Und in der Mitte mein Großvater, ein Auge auf die Welt
und eines nach innen gerichtet, vor sich ein Teller
Kartoffeln, mehlig und buttergelb, gut für Schweine
und Menschen und mich.

5

Das alles bin ich, der Mann mit dem Hasenherz.
Nicht mehr, eher weniger.

SCHATTEN UND LICHT

Ich kannte einen, der kannte nichts
Dunkleres als das Licht, das er ein Leben lang
untersuchte mit kurzsichtigen Augen.
Er vertiefte sich in den dichten Schatten
des Talmud und feilte wie ein Tagelöhner
an den bärtigen Schriften der Gnosis,
bis er selbst wie einer der Buchstaben aussah,
die Gott nicht erkennen.
Von ihm lernte ich, woher das Licht kommt
auf den Bildern Vermeers, das sich nie wiederholt.
Seine klugen, kurzen Essays über den Winkel,
die Ecke, den Schleier werden von Faltern gelesen,
die aus gelehrten Büchern aufsteigen,
sein Roman in Fragmenten bleibt unerhört.
Wir besuchten täglich den Brunnen, in den,
wie es heißt, die Magd gefallen war
beim Betrachten der Sterne, und nichts
konnte ihn stärker erschüttern als die Ameisen,
die den Erdball rotieren ließen.
Als die Kerze erlosch, in deren Schein
er all seine Schriften verfaßte, ergab er sich
endlich dem Licht, an das er nicht glaubte.

200

AUSZUG

Jetzt sind die Zimmer leer, die Koffer
stehen im Flur neben mürrischen Kisten,
in denen Bücher mit Zeitungen kämpfen.
Ein ungleicher Kampf: Papier gegen Papier,
die Fortsetzung einer alten Tragödie.

Wie stark die Leere riecht! Eine Fliege
dreht ihre Runden und fotografiert,
ein Engel mit schwarzer Fahne,
vernarrt in eine summende Liturgie.
Auf dem Fensterbrett eine Münze
der alten Währung, die alles bezahlt.

Kein Stuhl, kein Bett mehr bittet um Nachsicht,
sogar die Erinnerung hat sich verkrümelt
wie die Schaben. Hat hier einer gelebt?
Bald wird der Abend einziehen
und den Abdruck der Bilder löschen,
die wir abgehängt haben,
um sie nie wieder aufzuhängen.

ZWEI ROTE FISCHE, EIN SCHWARZER

Der Fischer keht zurück, in seinem Netz
zwei rote Fische, ein schwarzer.
Er schenkt mir den Fang der Nacht.
Jetzt flickt er in sein zerissenes Netz
tausend silbrige Leiber. Ich lese.
"Mit Bild", lese ich, "meinen wir alles,
das als Vermittlung dient, um Zugang
zu etwas anderem zu gewinnen."
Das Ufer fliegt weg, der Traum.
Mit seinen knotigen Fingern reißt er
den Himmel auf, die wahre Heimat,
und zeigt mir die letzte der traurigen
Utopien.

NÄCHTLICHE EINKEHR

Wir kehrten ein. Über dem Tisch
hing ein klebriger Fliegenfänger
mit tausend toten Geschichten.
Der Wirt war sprachlos, zu essen
gab es nichts. Einer von uns
sagte: Wir, wir sind noch weit weg
vom Leben. Wir ließen die Flasche
kreisen, sie zeigte auf mich.
In der Ferne konnte man
das sanfte Brummen der Autobahn
hören, es kam immer näher.
Wenn ich mich nicht irre,
sind wir nicht heil geblieben.

ANGEKOMMEN

Die Stadt ist fast leer.
An den Tankstellen im Zentrum
wird nur noch Haß abgegeben
gegen eine unbekannte Währung.
Gras und Brennesseln
belagern die Zapfsäulen,
deren Zählwerke eine Sprache üben,
die hier keiner versteht.
Der Tankwart will uns
stumm eine Lektion erteilen.
Er starrt angestrengt
in den Himmel, als bemühe er sich,
dort etwas zu lesen.
Kurz ist unser Schatten
unter der hochstehenden Sonne.

BRÜCKE

Nur eine schmale Brücke, die das Dunkel
mit dem Dunkel verbindet. Und ein Licht,
das die Welt auflöst in winzige Punkte,
die wir mühsam miteinander verbinden,
um ein Bild zu erhalten – als hätten wir
ein Recht auf ein Bild mit festem Rahmen.
Von Norden wehen unverständliche Sätze
über den Steg, Kindheitsworte, in Honig
getaucht und in den Wind gehalten,
die wollen uns treffen, hier, auf der Brücke,
die das Dunkel mit dem Dunkel verbindet.
Unter uns nimmt das Wasser den Kieseln
die Schärfe, damit sie weiterkommen
und sich auflösen können im Meer.
Wie winzig ist die Brücke, die deine Augen
verbindet – sie ist wie ein Schrei
über der wortlosen Angst, nicht mehr.

ENGLISCHER GARTEN

Ein Stirnrunzeln huscht
über das nachdenkliche Land,
der Sommer tritt ab,
in der Uniform eines Offiziers.
Insekten reizen die Wörter
zu religiösem Geschwätz,
Schafe stehen herum,
als hätte sie einer verloren,
und die Nacht fällt
wie ein Bussard aus dem Himmel.
Zurück bleibt eine Gruppe
Versprengter, die nicht weiß,
was sie in sich trägt,
sie bittet den Tod ins Gras.

BESUCH AUF DEM FRIEDHOF

Ein Grab wird geöffnet, mit beiden Beinen
stehen die Arbeiter in der Grube, sie schauen
aus der Tiefe zu mir hoch. Langsam wird
das Verborgene sichtbar, von roten Händen
ans Licht gebracht. Klumpige Erde, Schnecken,
Holz und ein paar Knochen, nichts, was uns
schrecken könnte. Hatte ich mehr erwartet?
Als Kind wollte ich wissen, was alles
mit den Toten verschwindet und nie wieder
auftaucht, die heiligen Dinge des Lebens.
Ich gehe weiter, mein Schatten sucht
auf eigene Rechnung nach anderen Toten,
wie ein Schlafwanderer balanciert er
auf dem grünen Grat zwischen den Gräbern.

ENDE DES SOMMERS

Länger werden wieder die Briefe
ans Licht, auf leichtsinnige Blätter
gestochen; die Erzählungen wandern
mit der Sonne, leicht und gesprächig,
verrauscht ist das zweideutige Fest.
Die Welt der Möglichkeiten wächst
mit dem Schatten. Nur einer sagt:
Es bleibt, wie es war.
Wie ein Dieb zerrt der Wind
an unseren Kleidern, und das Wasser
hat keine Zeit mehr für Diskretion.

DIE FRAU, DIE LIEST

Wenn ich an dich denke, sehe ich
eine Frau, die im Schatten liest.
Sie verbirgt eine Sprache unter der Zunge,
die das Dunkel nicht meidet.
Sie liest so leise, daß ich es höre:
"Sie lächelten mir zu, wie Tote lächeln,
wenn sie sehen, daß wir denken,
sie seien nicht mehr am Leben."
Die Buchstaben stehen auf vor ihr
und verlassen das Buch, das sie liest,
in dem Augenblick, da ich an dich denke.

DAS KREUZ

In den alten Kirchen im Süden
schlage ich manchmal das Kreuz,
um das Gespräch mit dem Heiligen
zu erleichtern. Es wirkt. Ich rede
dann lange mit den salpetrigen Engeln,
die in den feuchten Ecken leben,
in einem Gemisch aus Demut
und Orthodoxie. In Barcelona,
im Dom, verließ die heilige Milena
ihr verstaubtes Fresko, eine junge Frau,
und setzte sich zu mir
auf die kalten Marmorstufen des Altars.
Wir mußten flüstern. Um uns herum
alte Damen, die statt des Rosenkranzes
ihre Einkaufsnetze hielten. Es roch
nach Minze, Weihrauch, Apfelsinen.
Milena zeigte auf einen Wanderer
auf einem dunklen Bild, der einen Blitz
anstarrte, eine zuckende Natter am Himmel.
Das wirst du sein, sagte sie, du wirst
diesen Weg gehen müssen, aber keine Angst,
ich werde hier auf dich warten.

LETZT FRAGEN

Mein Haus hat sechs Türen,
alle aus gutem Holz.
Die erste verhandelte zu lange
mit dem Architekten über den Platz,
der ihr zukomme, und wurde geschlossen.
Die zweite ist allergisch gegen Licht
und läßt sich bei Tag nicht öffnen.
Die dritte steht nur im Traum offen
und zeigt einen alten bärtigen Engel,
der seine Pflicht tut.
Die vierte führt in eine heile Welt
und wird nicht mehr benutzt.
Die fünfte sucht ihre Form
nach dem alten Maßstab des Möglichen.
Die sechste ist unsichtbar.
Seit Jahren fahre ich mit den Händen
die Wände ab, um sie endlich zu finden.
Ich weiß genau, daß sie existiert.
Natürlich wäre es möglich,
dem Haus eine weitere Tür zu verpassen,
wie alle Freunde mir raten.
Aber lieber reiße ich das Haus ab,
um in den Trümmern Eingang zu finden.

ZU SPÄT

Es ist schon nach Mitternacht,
die Zeiger der Uhr atmen durch.
Eine Schnecke macht sich auf
und nimmt die aschgrauen Worte mit,
bis das Papier wieder weiß ist,
eine Landkarte der Leere.
Mir bleibt keine Zeit.
Wie Wasser, das im Frühjahr
aus dem Stein tritt, sickert
das Frühlicht herein.
Hellwach gehe ich schlafen.

RAST

Der See ist zugewachsen, und eine Stille
nistet im Schilf, als sei die Lektion
gelernt und begriffen: kein Wort mehr
über die verlorene Zeit. Nur die Binsen
nicken wie jüdische Beter, eine traurige Utopie
der Bewegung. Das Wasser zieht sich zurück,
der Himmel hängt tief und schwer
über den Wiesen, und ein blasser Mond
wagt sich aus den aschgrauen Wolken.
In der Stadt tobt ein Krieg, man sieht,
wie das Feuer sich an der Dunkelheit mißt.
Doch das ist noch lange nicht alles.

WIE WAR'S?

Wir saßen zu lange zusammen, wie immer
wenn es um Kunst und Leben geht.
Jeder hatte etwas zu sagen,
jeder hielt etwas zurück.

Einer stand auf. Stand mit beiden Füßen
zwischen Erde und Himmel, wort-
und hilflos, als wollte er
seine Ohnmacht beweisen.

Über uns – wir saßen im Garten -
bildeten die Vögel eine zitternde Leiter,
die leicht und beweglich
in den Wolken verschwand.

ZUR LAGE

So wie die Dinge sich entwickeln
ist es Zeit, Pläne zu machen
für das Jahr und das Jahr davor.
Ein Buch muß gelesen werden,
die Quote für Mitleid gesenkt werden.
Wir wollen nicht aus Irrtum sterben,
sagen wir und schütteln den Kopf.
Unsere Ängste sind Mißverständnisse,
das stimmt, sagen die andern.
Was stimmt? Im Dunkeln suchen wir
in den alten Wörterbüchern
nach der exakten Bedeutung von Glück.

NACHTS

Wenn der Schlaf sich ächzend
von Zimmer zu Zimmer schleppt,
flüstern die wachen Stunden
mit dem wildfremden Mond.
Jetzt müßte ein Boot ablegen
in dem mausgrauen Himmel,
weit weg von aller Menschenwärme.

GANZ KURZ VOR DEM GEWITTER

Ein sanfter Regen, und die Zeder,
in den Abend gestickt mit tausend Stichen
und einem, verliert ihre Fassung.
Auch die Steine machen sich auf,
sie suchen ein Ufer. Nur die Saatkrähen
mit ihren nackten weißlichen Gesichtern
beschließen zu bleiben. Sie zerren
an dem Tuch, das die Dinge verhüllt,
als gelte es etwas zu zeigen.
Alles noch Sichtbare erinnert sich
an das Unsichtbare, das immer und ewig
unsichtbar bleibt, wenn das Gewitter
hereinbricht.

REALITY SHOW

für Peter von Matt

Im Garten leben jetzt Wölfe.
Mit Rührung schauen wir zu,
wie sie ihre blutigen Pfoten lecken.
Ihr Geruch breitet sich aus wie Gas.

Einer hat eine Ente unter den Krallen,
ein andrer zwei Amseln. Pechvögel.
Wir fragen die Natur um Rat,
aber die Sonne hält sich bedeckt,

und der Regen hat sich ins Zentrum verzogen.
Hungrige Tiere. Ihre Augen leuchten
wie Tinte und Blut. Nachts liegen sie
unter dem Apfelbaum und knirschen

laut mit den Zähnen.

TO WHOM IT MAY CONCERN

Auch wenn es sich nicht ziemt,
blicken wir gerne zurück: die Straßen
werden schmaler, die Häuser kleiner,
das große Thema löst sich zusehends auf.
Mit einer Welt im Rücken lebt es sich
leichter, der Krieg wird ein Spiel,
selbst das Blut ist nichts weiter
als rote Farbe auf einem Bild.
Wir bewundern das kräftige Blau
über dem anderen Ufer. Fromm zu sein
blieb uns leider ersparrt, der Ruf
der Blumen, der Äcker, des Wegrands,
nicht mehr der Rede wert.
Die Briefe, die uns das Unglück geraubt,
zeigen eine dummes Bedürfnis nach Klarheit.
Schau, die Prozession der Ameisen,
ihrer gefräßigen Neugier kann nichts
widerstehen.

PASSAGE

Der Schnee begann zu rauchen,
ein bläulicher Schleier lag über dem Weiß.
Wir kamen nicht mehr vorwärts,
sirrend drehten die Räder durch.
Einer schrieb in sein Tagebuch:
Um uns herrscht zögerndes Trauern.
Manche versuchten gehend ihr Glück,
ihre Schatten kamen mühelos
am Mondlauf über den Berg.

BEWERBUNG

Ich habe nichts zu verbergen:
die Müdigkeit ist angeboren,
die Augen schon immer eine offene Wunde,
mein Lebenslauf ist verlorengegangen
auf früheren Arbeitsstellen.
Mein Ich nennt die Neigung,
sich aufzulösen, einen Sieg
der Trauer über den Schmerz.
Mein einziges Geheimnis
ist zahm wie ein alter Hund,
es tut keinem weh und bleibt
fremden Blicken entzogen.
Ich bin noch zwanzig Jahre tauglich,
danach nur bedingt.
Es bleibt ein Rätsel,
daß Menschen zusammenleben,
ohne Nachsicht zu bitten
für diesen unhaltbaren Zustand.

POETIK, SEPTEMBER 1998

für Wulf Segbrecht

I

Goethes Geburtstag vorüber, und die Kurse fallen
ins Bodenlose. Der Dollar ist zur Bückware geworden.
Die Schnee-und Schmerzgrenze liegt bei 1300 Metern,
wir hier am Flachland leben bereits unter Wasser.
Veba, Fontane, Rheinstahl, alles fällt, Novalis
wird nicht mehr notiert. Wo steht eigentlich Celan?
Auch die Klassik ist angeblich ins Rutschen geraten,
Karajan, Celibidache, die großen Geigenvirtuosen,
alles Namen, die keiner mehr kennt. Dafür soll Dr. Kohl
in Bayeuth den Ring ins nächste Jahrhundert tragen
helfen. Nur die Autoindustrie boomt gewaltig,
seit sie Fluchtautos herstellt, die am Zielort
zerfallen. Nichts als Regen. Selbst im Parlament
riecht es nach nasser Wolle. Im Keller in Bonn
wollen sie jetzt Pilze züchten, heißt es
aus gewöhnlich gut unterrichteten Kreisen: denn
die Wirtschaft ist unser Schicksal. Unser Mandala.
Zwangsarbeiter werden nun mit Verspätung bezahlt,
aber sie sollen sich ordentlich anstellen bitte.

2

Es wird immer leichter, sich eine Welt vorzustellen
ohne Menschen. Alles, was in den Schädel paßt,
in die weißen Lamellen links und rechts,
bliebe: die Reste auf dem Teller, der Sonnenstrahl.
durch das Schlüsselloch, der kleine dunkle Name
für die Liebe, das bronzegelbe Moos am Pantheon,
ein paar dem Gedächtnis abgebettelte Verse.
Du wachst auf von einer eisigen Kälte und entdeckst,
daß der Tod neben dir schläft, mit offenen Augen.
Du könntest alle versteckten Werte freilassen,
weil sich keiner mehr von ihnen rühren ließe.
Ständig würdest du an Türen klopfen, hinter denen
Menschen lebten, manchmal wäre noch der Fernseher
zu hören, sein helles Rauschen. Hier z. B. wohnte
der Gegner. Seit auch er dich verlassen hat,
gibt es nur noch Siege. Überall Unkraut, ein herrliches Wuchern
in verwahrlosten Gärten. Lange müßige Spaziergänge
in Begleitung von Schnecken, Amseln und Hasen.
Wie höflich die Tiere sind! Wie zuvorkommend! Nietzsche

haben sie gelesen, Platon und Kant. Und sie fragen dich
allen Ernstes, wo denn die Menschen geblieben sind?
Irgendwann kommst du ans Meer.
Von weitem schon siehst du die leeren Schiffe,
wie sie sich voreinander verbeugen, den grauen Strand
unter einem grauen Himmel. Ein paar alte Sandalen,
jetzt von Krebsen bewohnt, eine Plastikflasche, mehr
ist nicht zu finden. Du würdest dich hinhocken
und ein Gedicht schreiben in den Sand, wie so viele
von dir, aber in rechter Entfernung zum Wasser,
dein Beitrag für die Unsterblichkeit.

3

Ein Engel sitzt im Garten und weint,
weil sich das Unglück nicht auf Unglück reimt.

ÜBER TRÄUME

Mein Großvater, ein nüchterner Bauer
mit trockenen Händen wie Schmirgelpapier,
behauptete, er träume grundsätzlich
die Träume von anderen.
Es war eine ärmliche Zeit, der Krieg
hatte um den Hof herum seine schweren Waffen
liegengelassen, und viele hatten vergessen,
was sie vergessen hatten.
Man konnte auf fast alles verzichten,
auf Fragen, Kaffee und auf Wärme.
Auch auf Wünsche, um die Ruhe der Welt
nicht zu stören. Aber daß einer
allen Ernstes behauptete,
auf die eigenen Träume verzichten zu können,
das war auch bei uns ein starkes Stück.

UNVERHOFFTES WIEDERSEHEN

Wir kannten uns zu einer Zeit,
als uns die Helligkeit noch gehörte.
Damals schrieben wir dunkle Gedichte
über die Invasion des Lichts,
die wir auswendig lernten.
Und jeden Abend machten wir
einen Ausflug auf das verlassene Gelände
der Philosophie, vor unserer Haustür.
Wir trafen uns wieder im Postamt.
Er wollte einen Brief loswerden,
den er damals geschrieben hatte,
ich suchte nach seiner Telefonnummer.
Die Schlange nahm uns auf
und trennte uns durch eine Frau mit Kind,
die sich aufgeben wollten.
Ein ungewöhnlich heißer Sommer
zog uns die Erinnerung vom Leib.
Der Rest paßte auf eine Ansichtskarte.

DAS SCHÖNE

für Charles Simic

Vor dem Parkhaus saß einer
auf einem umgedrehten Eimer
und fragte mich rücksichtslos
nach dem Begriff des Schönen.
Die Sonne schien ernsthaft
in sein müdes Gesicht.
Etwas, was sich nur schwer
miteinander verträgt, wollte ich
sagen, blieb aber stumm
und legte ihm ein Geldstück
auf die Hand, die nicht losließ.
Wir tranken Bier aus der Büchse.
Über uns das heisere Geschrei
der Krähen in einem Lindenbaum,
das trotz der ernsten Fragen
nicht verstummen wollte.

REDE DES BETRÜBTEN

Ich bin er Betrübte.
Alle Versuche, mich aufzuheitern,
schlugen fehl.
Warum lachst du nicht,
fragen die Menschen.
Worüber, antworte ich,
Ich will mit der Hoffnung
nicht verhandeln.
Weil ich schlaflos bin,
gehe ich nachs spazieren.
Ich höre die Tiere atmen,
die Schatten flüstern mir zu.
Einmal fand ich … doch
darüber will ich nicht reden.

MAX SEBALD IST TOT

Ein Schriftsteller ist gestorben,
mitten im Text.
Um uns zu trösten,
müssen die anderen schweigen,
aber nicht für immer,
aber sofort.

NACHRUF AUF EINEN DICHTER

Er erhob sich vor unseren Augen
von seinem Totenbett, um ein Komma
zu setzen, dann schlief er ein.
Sein Werk ist heute vergessen.

REDE DES HISTORIKERS

Ich habe, was ich fassen konnte,
aus der Geschichte in der Gegenwart geschleppt.
Ich habe Akten gelesen, Dokumente studiert,
mit den Barbaren geredet
und ihren Feinden, unseren Freunden.
Mein Bleistift ist nur noch ein Stummel,
der Radiergummi verbraucht, das Tintenfaß
leer. Ich wollte herausfinden, warum wir sind,
wie wir sind.
Als mein Werk abgeschlossen war,
glich es einem dunklen Spiegel.
Ich erschrak nicht einmal, als ich
hineinsah und mich erblickte,
unendlich mißglückt.

DAS ELFTE GEBOT

Du sollst
nicht sterben,
bitte.

Unter freiem Himmel

from *MEDITATIONEN UNTER FREIEM HIMMEL*

*

Die Helligkeit ist endlich bereit,
sich dem Dunkel zu öffnen,
wie eine höhere Mechanik es befiehlt.
Vom Wald her höre ich
das trockene Husten der Rehe,
in der kupfernen Dämmerung
lösen die letzten Bindungen sich auf.
Es gibt keine Regeln,
an die man sich halten darf,
das ist die Botschaft
aus der rasenden Zeit.
Über mir, im kindlichen Himmel,
steht ein Hubschrauber,
Armee oder Archäologie, das ist jetzt egal.
Früher haben hier Menschen
gesiedelt; manchmal treten sie
noch heute im Dunkel aus dem Wald
und klappern ihren alten Knochen.
Der Boden hat Hitze gehortet.
Die Erinnerung geht in Sprüngen,
damit Ihre Füße nicht verbrennen.

*

Eben noch standen wir lachend
unter den Kandelabern der Tannen
und bewunderten den silbrigen Frost,
der die Äste bekleidete, da fiel
plötzlich Nebel. Immer unvollständiger
war nun der Himmel, die Bilder
schmolzen vor unseren Augen. Wie Rauch
war die Atmosphäre, undurchdringlich
und weich. Wir blieben angewurzelt
stehen und warteten auf das Urteil.

*

Hundertmal übt der Pirol
das Unglück der Meisterschaft.
Dann stürzt er eilig davon,
ein gelber Riß im Universum,
der nie mehr verheilt.

*

Große schwarze Vögel
besetzen seit Tagen das Land.
Sie nehmen uns, ungerührt,
das Wort aus dem Mund.
Was wollten wir erzählen?
Davon, wer wie sein wollten,
bevor Mord und Totschlag
unsere Nachbarn wurden,
einer links, einer rechts.
Jetzt verlieren wir wortlos
die Zeit. Die Vögel, ungerührt
reden sich ein in ihre
schwarze Welt.

*

Im Teich die reglosen Molche,
von Wasserspinnen umkreist,
sie ersetzen die Uhr. Eine Maus
ist ertrunken. Wespen bilden
eine Jakobsleiter, damit ihre Seele
aufsteigen kann. Einen Segen,
heißt es, kann man nicht widerrufen.
Aber was gibt uns das Recht,
fast alles zu verraten, um uns
zu retten. Ach, wie ich die Nacht
herbeisehne, die gute Nacht des Denkens,
wenn die Geschichte schläft.

Naturstück

Über dem Horizont steht ein Vogel.
Er sieht den Hasen, der über die Wiese fliegt,
die Zeit macht sich aus dem Staub
eine Maus im unsterblichen Unkraut.
Jede Ameise sieht er, die bewegliche Summe
der Schlaflosigkeit. Er sieht kleinere Vögel,
deren Geschrei die Mauern aufweckt.
Er sieht auch uns, feine aufrechte Tiere,
denen die Wahrheit am Herzen liegt.
Er sieht, wie wir den Mund aufreißen.
Man kann keine Rede mehr sein.

*

Wir lernen nichts mehr hinzu,
das war das Ergebnis eines Kongresses
auf der anderen Seite der Welt.
Keiner wußte, ob er traurig sein sollte,
weil es jeder geahnt hat.
Schwalben, dünn wie Kompaßnadeln,
bleiben tagelang in der Luft.
Uns mißlingt alles, fast alles.
Wir können nicht verhindern, daß der Fluß
das Licht stromabwärts führt,
und nachts prallen Insekten auf Augen und Mund,
wenn wir fassungslos in der Nacht stehen,
am anderen Ende des Wachens.
Gottlob haben wir nur eine schwache Ahnung
von dem, was wir sind, das wäre das Ende.

*

Aufrecht kamen wir an,
Ein Häuflein Bewunderer
der Unfertigkeit, ließen Schnee
unserer Vorstellungen färben,
Brombeeren unseren Schmerz.
Wir packen zu,
Bis die Müdigkeit unsere Gesichter
polierte, atmeten ein, atmeten aus
und mußten schon wieder gehen.

Sommer

Wir wollen glücklich sein. Über uns der Ahorn,
winkend mit tausend Händen, und darüber
ein vermummter Himmel, mit allen Rollen
zufrieden und fähig zum Irrtum.
Grillen zersägen den Schatten. Und Mücken
weben an des Sommers Totenmaske.
ein Eichelhäher gibt lachend Befehle:
Nimm es nicht hin! Es dauert Jahre,
bis die Botschaft gehört wird: zu viel
geht zu Ende, zu wenig beginnt.

DICHTER ZU BESUCH

Er kommt unangemeldet, wie immer,
und erzählt die Geschichte vom Fluß,
der seinem Namen entgegenfließt,
ihn aber nie erreicht.

Ich bin der Fluß, sagt der Dichter,
als hätten wir es nicht längst gewußt.
Alles steckt er ein, man muß aufpassen,
sein Appetit auf Dinge ist unersättlich.

Was ihn an Würde erinnert oder
Verehrung beansprucht, ist ihm peinlich,
dann redet er über Wasserflöhe und Schilf.

Drei Tage fließt er durch unser Haus,

und drei Tage schauen wir uns an,
ohne zu wissen, wer wir sind.

SAG DEN SPERBERN
für Wolfgang Bächler

Sag den Sperbern,
sie sollen die Uhr mir
stellen nach meinem Tod,
und der Falke, mein Freund,
soll das Zifferblatt spalten,
bevor der Blitz es trifft.
Ein Satz verbirgt sich
in jeder Freundschaft,
der kommt nie
zur Sprache,
nie.
So stand es auch
zwischen uns.

EIN FREUND

In einem Hotel wollte er leben, am Meer,
täglich mit anderen Menschen frühstücken,
die ihm ihre Träume aufs Brot schmieren,
während er stumm sein Vierminutenei köpft.
Keine Bücher, keine Post, keine Gewißheiten,
und wenn die Putzfrau das Zimmer
verlassen hat: eine Seite schreiben
und rein in den Umschlag, Absender
ist wieder mal nicht das Hotel.

Er starb in der Stadt, im Altenheim,
die Ohren verstopft gegen schöne Worte.
Seine Notizbücher und Kladden,
die wir in seinem Nachlaß fanden,
berichten von der Freundschaft zu Schwalben
und den täglichen Besuchen des Todes.
Eine Seite ist der Grasnelke gewidmet,
Armeria vulgaris, der Schönheit abhold,
nicht mal als Tee zu genießen.

SPAZIERGANG

mit Richard Pietraß

Auf der Höhe: keine Sicht,
die Welt ist ausgestorben.
Früher sprachen wir von Heiligen,
aber wie sehen sie heute aus?
War der Aufstieg vielleicht
doch nur ein Abstieg?
An den Flüssen zurück.
Warum sollte das Wasser sich sorgen,
das dem Unglück vorauseilt
in die Nachmittage, den Abend?
Was wir nicht mehr brauchen,
nimmt die Pappel auf,
die geduldige, die nicht fragt,
was wir brauchen.
Wer glaubt, was er sagt,
wenn er lügt, der trete vor,
danach kann es dunkel werden.

SO WIE FRÜHER GEDICHTE DIE WELT ERHELLEN SOLLTEN

So wie früher Gedichte die Welt erhellen sollten,
die es nicht gab, den Weg, vom Ginster behütet,
von der silbrigen Distel, den Fluß und den Rückfluß,
den verschlossenen Himmel, von weißen Vögeln
zerrissen; so wie später Gedichte den hellen Streifen
Licht unter der Tür festhalten sollten,
die erstarrte Woge der Schrift, das Herz,
ausgedörrt von der Fürsprache heftiger Worte;
so wie kürzlich Gedichte aussprechen sollten,
was wir uns nicht aneignen konnten, die Verfinsterung,
das unbewohnbare Dunkel als Bedingung des Lichts,
den Zufall als Gesetz der Wahrscheinlichkeit;
so müssen sie jetzt zu sich selber sprechen
in einer Sprache, die ihnen nicht gehört,
in der wir uns selbst nicht vergessen.

WIR HATTEN UNS VERABREDET

Wir hatten uns verabredet,
nachts, zwischen den Dörfern,
unter dem abnehmenden Mond.
Sie wollte ihr Pferd mitnehmen,
ich schleppte den Koffer.
Ich hatte mir jedes Wort überlegt.
Sie sollten leicht sein, aber nicht vage,
bestimmt, aber nicht zu schwer.
Das Wort Liebe lernte ich auswendig,
um es nicht gebrauchen zu müssen.
Auf der Höhe der Zypressen,
die wie Dochte in der Erde steckten,
gingen wir grußlos aneinander vorbei.

MEIN GROßVATER, CHRISTLICH ERZOGEN

Mein Großvater, christlich erzogen,
liebte die sanftmütigen Sterne.
Nur die Kometen, die Wunden rissen
in das feine Tuch des Himmels,
verabscheute er aus ganzem Herzen.
Unruhestifter, Chaoten, brummelte er,
verschanzt hinter seinem Fernglas.
Die Großmutter, die ihm beistand,
mußte bis zum Morgengrauen
horchen, ob Kometen durchs Weltall
sausten, bis sie die Sonne ins Bett
trieb.

DAS IST DAS LETZTE BILD

Das ist das letzte Bild
von meinem Vater und mir.
Wir waren ans Meer gefahren,
hatten uns in einem Strandkorb gesetzt
und stundenlang übers Wasser geschaut.
Mein Vater sprach, wie er sonst
nie getan hatte. Schön wars
und peinlich, ihm zuzuhören.
Was er mir sagen wollte?
Keine Ahnung. Aber ich wußte,
es war lebenswichtig für uns beide.
Später hatte er etwas in den Sand
direkt am Wasser geschrieben,
weil er ahnte, daß die Wellen
den Text sofort wieder löschen würden.

DER APFELBAUM

wird geschnitten, noch hängen
zwölf Äpfel im Geäst.
Eine Krähe hält mir
den Tod vom Leib.
Die schweren Schritte des Denkens
im Gras.
Ich selbst habe Redeverbot.
Was nicht zur Sprache kam,
verwelkt lange im Schatten.

HOTEL FUTURE

Willkommen! Sind sie unterwegs,
um ein Unglück zu vergessen
oder tragen Sie es mit sich herum?
Der Portier hat ein Gesicht,
das der Kummer schon aufgegeben hat.

Ich kenne alle Zimmer auswendig.
In der Heizung wird die Ilias geflüstert,
nur die Sterbenden schreien vor Hitze.
Etwas, was noch zu tun bleibt:
Das Unrettbare retten.

Ich wohne im obersten Stockwerk,
bei den Tauben. Vor dem Fenster
erblüht ein fiebriger Himmel.
Die Zeit ist ins Land gegangen
zu den Steinen, die nie schlafen.

DAS LEERE HAUS

Wie eine Sakristei steht das leere Haus
vor der schweigenden Orgel der Ulmen.
Eine Schule, in der man lernen kann,
wie man Armut erzeugt. Ein Käuzchen
gibt den Ton an. Der Krieg geht ein
und aus, ohne zu fackeln. Es riecht
nach Bohnerwachs und frischem Zimt.
Die Schatten bleiben länger als erwünscht.
In der Ferne das gewaltige Lachen
der See. Und immer, wenn ich schlafen will,
beginnt der Chor mit der Probe.

SEPTEMBERLIED

Krähen, wie mit Blei gefüttert,
fallen auf die Straße.
Wir nehmen abergläubische Umwege,
um an Brot und Wein zu kommen.
Bald sehen wir wie Menschen aus,
die nicht zurückfinden wollen,
unsere Gesichter dunkeln ein,
als wären sie mit dicker Kreide
auf eine schattige Mauer gemalt.
Die Bücher verlieren Leser,
die Buchstaben fliegen einzeln davon,
Leim tropft schwer auf den Boden.
Wollen wir umkehren?
An den sauertöpfischen Krähen vorbei
nach Hause, am Zuhause vorbei?

WARUM HÄLTST DU DIE HÜHNER

"Warum hältst du die Hühner
Auf dem Dach?" fragte ich
den Großvater.
"Würden sie unten leben",
war seine Antwort,
"müßten sie Steine
fressen, hier oben fressen sie Licht."

FLIEßENDES

In diesem Landstrich gibt's zu wenig Wasser.
Großmutter stellte einen Krug mit Klatschmohn
auf den runden, abgeschabten Tisch,
die gelblich-roten Blütenblätter, müde schon
vom kurzen Weg herauf, zwei lange Treppen,
in der von Atemnot geballten Faust.
Fürs Wasser gab es keine Leitung,
in Kannen mußte ich es holen,
ohne einen Tropfen auf fremder Treppe
zu verlieren, drei Kannen für den Körper,
eine für die Suppe und die Teller.
Und ein Glas Wasser für die Zähne,
ein seltsam schroffes Liebespaar,
das jede Nacht in einem Glas zusammenfand.
Von Osten kamen die Gewitter. Warum von Osten?
Das Zwiegespräch von Blitz und Donner,
es fand bei offenem Fenster, in dem Garten
statt, der kürzlich noch dem Großvater gehörte;
und dann ein Regenguß, der leicht die Kannen füllte.
Und noch viel später, kurz vorm Schlafengehn,
die Tränen. Der Junge, der nicht sprach,
er starrte auf die Blütenblätter,
die um die Vase einen feurroten Kreis beschrieben.
In diesem Landstrich gibt's zu wenig Wasser!
Hydraulik hieß die Kunst, die ich erlernen sollte, nicht
das Heil und nicht Gemeinschaft.
Und fand nicht einmal Worte, das Wasser,
wie es damals war, nur im Umriß zu beschreiben.

DORFKINO

Die Tür zum Garten wurde aufgestoßen:
Vögel flogen auf, alberne Schwalben
und Rotkehlchen in vollem Ornat.
Dorfkino, bezahlt wurde mit Äpfeln
und aufgescheuerten Knien. Dann kam
der andere ins Bild, der, der man nicht
war, der Mann mit der Leiter,
der in die Erde stieg, noch lang war
sein Husten zu hören. Er hat sich
wahrscheinlich verirrt und kehrt
dort nach oben zurück, wo ihn keiner versteht.
Sein Porträt hing an Kirsche
und Pappel, bis es Ameisen Stück
für Stück wie ein kostbares Fresko
abtrugen und unkenntlich machten.
Nur die unverwüstlichen Nägel
steckten noch lange im blutenden Holz.
Am Abend, wenn das Licht gefaltet
war, Ecke auf Ecke, klopfte einer
an die vordere Tür, der hatte noch Dreck
am Stecken und unter den Schuhen.
Er brachte Gerüchte mit, versteckt
unter der Zunge, die tauschte er
ein gegen Brot. Laut Großmutter
war er früher ein Dichter, einer der den Blumen
Worte anhängt, bis ihre Köpfe brechen.
Ab '49 war das Kino geschlossen.

FERNSEHEN

Der Wind fluchte, und im Traum
gab es nur Hingestreckte und Tote.
Ein Auto suchte die Leiche der Stadt ab
und kehrte um in die Stille.
Wir lernten die wenigen Worte,
mit denen man zuhören kann.
Jetzt brennt die Stadt, und die Flammen
zittern wie die Hände eines Kindes.
Eine Landungsbrücke voller Spatzen
weist in die Zukunft, ein Schiff
fährt vorbei, es hat Lämmer geladen,
die davon träumten, Wölfe zu sein.

ERINNERUNG

Uralte Häuser, aufgereiht
an wißbegierigen Straßen.
Einer im Dorf behauptete,
Gefühle seien Geschwätz.
Nur nicht daran denken!
sagte mein Großvater, denn
jetzt kommt der Winter.
Wir gingen Fische fangen
vor dem Frost. Laß nur
die Leute reden, sagte er
mit einem langen Blick,
in dem Gefühle nur so zappelten.

DER KOMET

Ein Komet wird wieder sichtbar –
hell (wie ein lange vermißtes Wort)
rast er auf uns zu.
Er hat nichts zu befürchten.
Der Wind kämmt sorglos das Gras.
Und wir suchen Städte auf,
in denen wir nicht sterben möchten.

230

IN DEN SCHWEIZER BERGEN

Wie ein alter Freund trat der Nebel
auf uns zu, ein stummes, unerwecktes Material,
das uns nach seinen Wünschen formte.
Wir hatten keine Zeit, nach einem Weg
zu fahnden, Bäume gingen vorbei,
gemächlich, wie auf Zehenspitzen,
das Wurzelwerk um die flüsternden Kronen
geschlagen, und Steine, frisch der Erde
entstiegen, zeigten ihren bärtigen Reichtum.
Unparteiischer Nebel, der die Schönheit
des Unsichtbaren preist, den glucksenden Bach
und das schüchterne Piepsen der Vögel.
Nur wir, ohne Augenzwinkern, scheu und verloren,
wir wußten nicht weiter und sahen nur noch
die Hand vor den Augen im Nebel.

DIE LANGE NACHT

Die Nacht hört lange nicht auf,
und das Geschrei der Vögel, das uns früher
das Licht ins Zimmer brachte wie ein Geschenk,
läßt auf sich warten. Ganz in der Nähe wird
Schwärze gemahlen aus Zukunft und Zeit,
man hört ein stetes Summen ohne Inhalt und Form.
Der Müller schläft. In seinem uralten Bart
wimmeln finstre Geschichten, die prasseln
wie Feuer, Geschichten vom Krieg, die sich
wie von selber erzählen. Zu viel Vergangenheit
hat uns geweckt, jetzt sitzen wir frierend
am Tisch uns warten auf den erlösenden Blitz,
der uns sichtbar macht. Hört ihr die Welt?
fragt einer, aber wer, das ist nicht zu sehen.

ZU KALT WAR DAS HAUS

Zu kalt war das Haus,
mein hauchdünner Schlaf
konnte die Schindeln nicht wärmen.
Über den See war ich gerudert
mit den letzten Vögeln,
die hatte das Schweigen verjagt.

ES IST NICHTS PASSIERT

Es ist nichts passiert,
was sich aufschreiben ließe.
Nur ist die Welt manchmal
so groß, daß die Wörter
sich darin verlieren.
Dann gehe ich zum See
und schaue den Enten zu.
Wenn die Wellen, die sie
im Wasser bilden, das Ufer
erreichen, strecke ich mich
im hohen Gras aus und bin
nicht mehr zu finden.

DAS ORAKEL VON DELPHI

Die Grille, Königin der falschen Rede,
versteht kein Wort von dem,
was sie uns stundenlang predigt.
Und Mücken, die sich unbändig freuen,
daß Gott zu spät auf die Welt kam.
Ich weiß nicht, in wessen Namen,
auf wessen Geheiß ich spreche,
sagt das Orakel von Delphi.
In ihrer blassen Mottenrobe
wächst die Zukunft aus den Steinen
und schaut uns nicht einmal an.
Geschrieben sind alle Worte,
doch ausgesprochen wurden sie nie.

LETZTE REDE DES DIKTATORS

Man weiß zu wenig über sich.
Heute bin ich mir z. B. nicht sicher
und gebe Befehl,
alle Bilder, die mich zeigen,
zur Wand zu kehren
bis zum Widerruf.

17. Juni 1996

Da der Diktator bald darauf starb, ohne sich noch einmal begegnet zu sein von Angesicht zu
Angesicht, blieben die Bilder in allen Einrichtungen verkehrt herum hängen bis zum heutigen Tag.

Ins Reine

FLOHKRAUT

Manchmal denke ich an Flohkraut,
das, wenn ich mich recht erinnere,
in meiner Jugend an Grenzsteinen wuchs,
die zu eigenen Gunsten versetzt worden waren.

Darauf stand Todesstrafe in manchen Fällen.

Flohkraut, eine nicht besonders liebliche Pflanze,
die heute kaum mehr erkannt wird.
Aber sie existiert noch! Als ich kürzlich versuchte
mein Leben etwas zu ändern, sah ich sie blühen.

AUF DEM SEE

I
Die Zeit schwimmt achtlos
an uns vorbei,
gegen die Wellen, die sich
hinter dem Boot wieder treffen,
ohne nachtragend zu sein,
während wir in diesem Boot
sitzen und rudern,
auf einem Punkt zu am Ufer,
der kleiner wird
bei kürzer werdendem Abstand.

II
Über uns schludrige Wolken,
von einem närrischen Föhn
über den Himmel gejagt.
Erregt und streitsüchtig das Wasser,
und späte Vögel,
die über die Wellen flitzen.
Menschen liegen am Ufer
wie träge Sommerfliegen,
als wir abstießen vom Steg
lange vor dem Gewitter.

III
Wie Gras sieht das Wasser aus,
graues Gras, an der Wurzel gepackt.

TÜBINGEN, IM JANUAR

für Georg Braungart

Schneelos der Himmel,
in der Takelage der Reben
kommt der Tag ans Licht.
Lebensmüd arbeitet vor mir
das Holz vom vergangenen Jahr.
Wie totgeschlagen die Zeit,
wie geschwollen die Sprache.
Es mag Ihnen seltsam vorkommen,
aber auch Krähen haben ein Herz.
Das ist, in wenigen Worten,
die wahre Geschichte meines Lebens.

ÜBER SCHATTEN

Ich kannte die guten und die schlimmen Schatten,
die raumlosen Schatten der Träume, in denen Theologen
um einen Zankapfel streiten, und den Schatten,
den Fische werfen und eilige Fliegen.
Mein Großvater mischte Schatten in die Saat,
damit etwas wächst, was nicht umsonst ist,
und die Spreu sich vom Weizen nicht trennt.
Und einmal sah ich den Schatten von Vögeln,
der hing an den Steinen wie die Wolle am Strauch.
Ab heute wirft auch mein Schlaf einen Schatten
in die immer lichtloser werdende Welt.

AM MEER

I

Am Ufer winzige Feuer,
in denen Briefe verbrennen.
Liebesbriefe,
undatiert und unverständlich.
Ein Kiosk, blau angestrichen,
vor dem betongrauen Meer,
davor ein geldgieriger Stuhl.
Man ahnt, daß der Horizont
auch ohne uns wandert.
So sitzen wir uns gegenüber,
das Meer und ich,
das eine dem anderen
ein finsterer Spiegel,
und haben Redeverbot.

2

Der heilige Franziskus, heißt es,
habe eine Woche lang
vom Zirpen der Zikade leben können.
Und ich höre mir täglich
das Gebrüll der Wellen an.

3

Sind das Möwen
Über dem dunklen Wacholder,
nah bei den offenen Gräbern?
Früher gab es hier Störche,
die haben das Totenbuch geführt,
da war die Luft noch rein
überm Meer.

DIE WASSERLÄUFER

Der Himmel: flüssiger Granit,
und man erschrickt, wenn Vögel
sich aus dem Masse lösen
und ohne Flügelschlag in weiten Bögen
Kreise um dich ziehn.
Die Makellosigkeit erschüttert dich.

Ich bin am Ufer festgewachsen,
schau den Fischen zu, die unbekümmert
aus dem Wasser schnellen.
In einer Stunde wird es dunkel sein.
Jetzt sehe ich die Wasserläufer,
die in die tintenschwarze Tiefe starren.

Wie Mikroskope stehn sie auf der Oberfläche,
regungslos, in einer Stunde sind sie tot.

DIE VÖGEL

Die Vögel in meinem Garten
führen ein Fahrtenbuch.
Manchmal fliegen sie
bis an die Schmerzgrenze
und bringen Namen heim,
die zu schwer sind
für den Wind, der sie trägt.
Ich sammle sie auf
und lege sie aus
wie die Krumen Brot
für die Vögel.
Am Abend, nach Sonnenuntergang,
ist das Fahrtenbuch leer,
als wären sie nie geflogen

DIE KRÄHEN VON CORBARA
für H. B.

I

Zuletzt werden die Wunschzettel kleiner,
und oft ist die zittrige Schrift
nicht mehr lesbar, wenn man einsehen muß,
daß der eingeschlagene Weg den Verzicht
auf alle anderen Wege bedeutet.
Es ist immer noch dieselbe Schrift,
die unsere Wünsche gehalten hat, die namenlosen
und die an ein Ziel geketteten Wünsche,
nach denen die Welt anders aussehen sollte,
wie nach einem langen Regen, wenn man
vor die Tür tritt und sich empfangen fühlt.
Warum dauert es so lange, bis man einsieht,
daß es auf uns nicht ankommt?
Und warum sagt es uns keiner?
Früher legten wir Münzen auf die Gleise
und ließen die Bahn darüber sausen,
heute verlieren sie von selbst ihr Profil.

2

Ich weiß nicht, was ich mir wünschen soll.
Vielleicht will ich noch einmal den Weg nach Corbara gehen,
wenn ein Landwind die Blätter des Ölbaums
seewärts dreht und die Zypressen nicken läßt
wie müde Lehrerinnen; oder wenn er die Pinien
mit ihrem Hang zur Nachdenklichkeit schüttelt,
bis die Krähen in den dünnen Schatten fallen,
der höflich den Weg bedeckt – der übrigens nachts
hell aufscheint, wenn wir uns Mühe geben,
keine Spuren zu hinterlassen bis zum Meer.
Ja, die Krähen von Corbara, halb dem Land
und halb dem Meer zugehörig, demonstrieren sie
über die Steilklippe das Gleichgewicht der Welt.
Und wir, mit unserer Witterung für das Falsche,
aufrecht und verletzbar, schauen glotzend an.

3

Das Meer und ich, wir verstehen uns besser.
Einmal liegt ein zerfetzter Schuh am Strand, und eine Spur
führt zurück in die flüsternde Brandung. Wir pochen
auf das Sichtbare und hören nicht auf die
schweigsamen, verschwiegenen Sprachen.
Ein Strom großer Kraft dringt vom schwarzen Granit des Meeres
in mich ein und vertreibt die vielen Worte für Unglück.
Und dann die Krähen über Corbara, ihr heiseres Krächzen.

GNOSTISCHE ÜBUNG, KORSIKA

In den Pinien der Geheimbund der Krähen,
graue Weste überm schwarzen Kleid,
das Thema: Wie viele Fliegen müssen sterben,
bis die Welt wieder gerecht wird.

Auf dem Spielplan der Dämmerung:
Die Verwandlung der Steine in Licht.
Man fragt das Gras nicht, warum
es sich verbeugt gegen die Laune des Winds,

die Steine nicht nach ihrem Alter.
Zerfleddertes Strandgras, dein Stammeln
ist das wahre Zeichen der Erlösung,
die es ohne dich nicht gibt.

Ein Kreuz, aus Licht gegossen,
das tragen die Schafe zum Strand.
Oktober. Der Kreislauf des Jahres
hat die Dinge nicht zerstört:

der Schuh, die Flasche, das zerrissene Hemd,
alles liegt da, vor der Erlösung.
Ein Hund treibt die Wellen zurück,
sie führen die Buchstaben mit sich,

die ein Wort formen wollten.
Arkadien, befristetes Exil.
Ich las die Geschichte von Ben Asi,
der das Geheimis des Paradieses schaute

und starb.

SPÄTER SEPTEMBER

I

Schwere Wolken am Septemberhimmel,
und das Land streckt sich, sie aufzufangen,
die Häuser erheben sich, der Ahorn,
schwer von der Nacht, öffnet die Hände,
und das brackige Bächlein, eben noch
schleppte es sich dahin wie ein Gefangener,
murmelt sich Mut zu am Morgen.

2

Dann die Stille, die Zeit ist in mir
und träumt die Träume der Toten,
ohne Scheu vor dem Leben, das mißlingt.

3

So kam es, daß die Wahrheit sich verirrte
in mein Haus. Sie löschte das Gekritzel,
nahm das Elend fort für eine gute Stunde,
ließ sich nieder auf dem Scherbenhaufen,
den die Nacht mir hinterlassen hatte.

4

Nur die Katzen lassen sich nicht täuschen.
Sie laufen herum, als läge auch das Haus
schon in Trümmen.

USBEKISCHE NÄCHTE

Vor dem Präsidentenpalais
ein paar verschämte Bäume,
sie bewachen den Staub.
Frauen mit dattelfarbigen Augen
verkaufen Nüsse, alle Nüsse
sind Teil der Nation.
Und alles ist richtig und falsch.

EIN FREUND SPRICHT

Ich hatte Berlin vergessen, jetzt
sehe ich es mit einem anderen Blick.
Der Geräusch der Autos auf dem Kopfsteinpflaster
vor Sonnenaufgang, als würden Rüben gehackt.
Und die Flugzeugbahnen, die wie früher
meine Handlinien nachäffen,
als hätten sie mein Schicksal studiert.
Wie hieß unser Nachbar, der Sammler
überarbeiteter Wörter, die nicht ahnten,
was noch kommen würde, unvorbereitet
für das Leid, das sie ausdrücken sollten?
Sein Haus steht noch, im Garten
leben Füchse, als sei das heute normal.
Ich studiere den Atlas der Wolken,
ein Geschenk des gütigen Himmels,
bevor er sich verabschiedet hat.

IN BULGARIEN
für Penka Angelova

Die braunweißen Tauben von Rousse
ziehen die Dämmerung über den Fluß,
und an den Sandbänken, wo die Angler wachsen,
bauen die Möwen ein Haus aus Staub,
als käme es darauf noch an.
Auf der Höhe ein Maulbeerbaum.
Jeder Zweig, jedes Blatt zieht mich
in ein kyrillisches Gespräch über Wasser.
Ich weiß nicht, wonach ich suche.
Die Menschen schlafen in Wassermelonen,
sie pressen die Kerne aus ihren Augen.
Nur die Kinder schlafen hier nie,
sie folgen dem Wasser in ein dürres Land.

243

SOFIA, IM FEBRUAR

Klares Wetter auf dem Weg nach Sofia.
Von oben sieht man sehr schön
die Rauchsäulen, aus denen Kriege entstehen.

Das Flugzeug schüttelt sich über dem Balkan,
aber die Geschichte hält die Balance.
Herr Selbstverständlich neben mir schläft.

Beim Anflug die Krähenbäume von Boyadzhiev,
sie geben dem unglücklichen Himmel Glanz.
(Wenn ihr wissen wollt, wie Schönheit entsteht!)

Ich kaufe eine Zeitung, die ich nicht lesen kann,
und teile mein Geld mit einem Zigeuner.
An jeder Ecke sehe ich mir selber zu,

und dann beginnt das wirkliche Bulgarien.

NORDFRIEDHOF

Geschwätzige Steine.
Nur ein Grab
verschließt die Erzählung.
Da springt
ein Vergißmeinnicht ein
und redet den Tod
ins Blaue.

BAUGRUBE

Von Himmel kein Sterbeswörtchen mehr,
stumme Wolken, schweigsame Nachmittage,
ein schwaches und hasenfüßiges Licht.
Und hin und wieder – mit abgewandtem Gesicht –
ein Windstoß, der wie ein Schlafwandler
rücksichtslos über die Kreuzung stolpert.

Vor meinem Fenster die Baugrube,
ein Ort der Sammlung: Zerborstene Klinker,
eine Puppe mit eingeschlagenen Zähnen,
schlafloses Gerümpel und ein Fahrrad,
das sich seit Tagen in die Erde wühlt.
Keine Ahnung, wer die Grube ausgehoben hat.

Manchmal sieht man Menschen auf dem Grund,
sie sehen aus wie Zwerge, die mit dünnen Fingern
den Halt der regensatten Wände prüfen.
Einer von ihnen hat einen Taschenspiegel,
mit dem er die Wolken zu fangen versucht.
Man hört ihn Tag und Nacht schimpfen.

Er soll mein Nachbar werden, später,
wenn mir die Worte fehlen werden
für das Licht.

ZUGBEKANNTSCHAFT

Ungefragt zählt er auf,
was ihm wichtig ist im Leben.
Ein paar Bücher,
die ihm Beine machten;
eine Liebe,
die er nicht zeigen konnte,
ums Verrecken nicht;
die Orakel des Donners;
untergehende Sonnen;
Geruch nach frischem Holz;
eine Landkarte ohne Grenzen,
so groß wie eine Hand;
gute diplomatische Beziehungen
zu allen Tieren, zu allen;
Dinge die nichts sagen
und dennoch nicht schweigen;
winzige Götter,
winzig wie Ameisen.
Und so weiter bis Köln.
Fast zu viel für ein Leben.
Und dann steigt er aus
und vergißt uns.

UNVERARBEITETER STOFF

für Adam Zagajewski

Wie uralte Patriarchen stehen die Bäume
um mich herum, sanft und traurig
üben sie ihre orthodoxe Liturgie.
Die Unendlichkeit zittert in jedem Blatt.
Streng, mürrisch und gedankenlos
fährt der Wind in die Gräser,
die sich alles gefallen lassen.
Wirklich verstanden haben wir nichts.
Angeblich geht keine Erzählung verloren,
nur die Anweisung zur Lebensführung
ist flüchtig, auf freiem Fuß.
Das Furchtbare liegt hinter uns,
das ist eines der endlich gelüfteten Geheimnisse,
von dem wir erzählen müssen,
der Rest ist das,
was wir vergessen haben.
Was nicht zu beenden ist.

SPÄTER SOMMER

Lange stand ich im Schatten
unter den verschorften Zweigen der Linde.
Das Blechdach des Schuppens
krachte unter der Hitze,
und die Himbeeren, vom Fuchs berührt,
sandten schwache Signale:
Uns darfst du nicht pflücken.
Der späte Sommer im Sprung erstarrt,
starrte mich weizengelb an.
Warum gibt es gute Gründe,
das Schlechte nicht zu verachten?
Ich nahm mir Stein um Stein
vom Herzen und schenkte sie
den kleinen Göttern, die im Grase
Karten spielten und auf Kundschaft hofften.
Ich stand so lange, bis der Nebel
mir die Beine wegriß und ich
nicht mehr wußte, wo ich mich
suchen sollte.

DER WEG

Ruhiger Abend. Ich gehe langsam,
laß den Weg, den kurzen, an mir
vorüberziehen, seinem Ende zu.
Die graue Traurigkeit der Buchen.
Ein Wille, der lange sich nicht brechen ließ,
ist längst gebrochen, und der Schotter
unter meinen Füßen erinnert sich
nicht mehr an das harte Geröll,
das einst hier niederging. Grashüpfer
mit Frisch gebügelten Flügeln
und Schwärme von Schmetterlingen
wie zarter Rauch über der frischen Mahd.
Mein Großvater wußte, wann und wie
der Schnitt zu machen ist, damit neues Leben
entstehe und das Gespräch nicht ende,
wenn er den Garten verlassen mußte.
Grauschwarz wie ein Maulwurf
steht ein Gewitter über dem Hang,
der Weg geht ungerührt weiter.

GLEICHZEITIGKEIT

Wetter: gesund,
und überm Holzzaun
Himbeergezwitscher.
Feinsliebchen opfert
ihr Ringlein der Elster
und stirbt.
Dann beginnt schon
der Flug der Krähen
im friedlosen Licht,
und die Herzzeitlose
blüht den Sommer
aus.

2009

für Remco Campert

Die Ernte ist abgeschlossen
im Versmaß des Sommers,
der Wind spricht schon leiser
mit der Stimme der Krähen.
Die Birke, mit schmächtigen Schultern,
diktiert ihr Journal dem ausgemergelten Licht:
Heut trug ich den Habicht!

Nichts wird ersetzt. Auch der Abend
verwandelt sich nicht mehr in Wissen.
Wir gehen auf Abwegen,
wo nur noch die Steine grüßen,
und jeder Stein erinnert sich heftig,
als wäre er nichts ohne uns.
Das wollte ich dir sagen,
bevor du von andern es horst.

LEERES FLUßBETT

So wie die Flüsse, die sich davonmachen
aus ihren Betten und einen Haufen
ratloser Steine zurücklassen,
so stehen wir an einem alten Morgen
vor dem bekritzelten Papier
und versuchen die Geheimschrift zu lösen.
Auch die Steine schreiben Geschichte.
Man muß sie nur so legen, daß später,
in der Zeit der Schmelze, die Schrift
sichtbar wird unter dem aufschäumenden Wasser.

ZWIELICHT

Ein Füchslein quert die Straße
und färbt den Waldrand rot.
Dahinter aufgebrochene Felder,
als hätte einer den Einstieg gesucht.
Keine Spur führt zur Biegung zurück,
wo das Füchslein verschwand.
Ich müßte umkehren, sofort,
doch meine Hand, die unwissende,
läßt ein Manöver nicht zu,
als hätte ich ein Gelübde getan,
an der Wahrheit vorbeizufahren.

DIE MÜCKE

Vielleicht ist es übertrieben,
der Mücke ein Denkmal zu setzen.
Aber auch sie hat, durch mein Blut,
Anteil an der Urgeschichte der Angst

BRIEF OHNE ABSENDER

Jemand schickt mir Fotos,
die uns zeigen, ihn und mich.
Eine Geschichte, die sich erzählt,
ohne daß ich sie verstehe,
als würde mir der Prozeß gemacht
in einem verjährten Verfahren.
Eine Geschichte aus der Geschichte
der Not, die auf etwas hinaus will:
Ich wollte nicht sein, wer ich war,
und will nicht sein, der ich bin.
Im Hintergrund ein Mädchen,
blond und spindeldürr, mit Schorf
auf den spitzen Knien, steil
in den Himmel starrt sie statt
direkt in ein flüchtiges Leben.

SABAS ZIEGE

Wenn ihr mich fragtet
nach meinem Lieblingstier,
ich würde Sabas Ziege nennen,
die mit dem trotzkistischen Bärtchen.
So stelle ich mir den Engel vor,
wenn er aus dem Dunkel tritt.
Wir trafen uns auf dem Karst,
wo der Wind nicht mehr Gewicht hat
als der Schatten.
Sie glaubte an das junge Geißblatt,
ich an das unabänderliche Gras.
Wir schrieben uns Briefe,
ihre Adresse ein verlassener Stall.
Manchmal begegnen wir uns
in zerfledderten Anthologien,
da steht sie hinter den Grillen,
ich bei den Krähen.
Zwischen uns eine Leere,
die nicht zu füllen ist.

LETZTER ZUG

Einer kam langsam auf mich zu,
den Hut in der Stirn,
die Hand über den Augen,
ein Dichter außer Dienst.
Auf seinem T-Shirt stand:
Ich spreche die paradiesische Sprache.
Er ging durch mich hindurch
und nahm den letzten Zug,
der für mich bestimmt war.
Keine Ahnung, was aus mir
geworden wäre. Von der Wahrheit
kennen wir nur den lausigen Kern.

DER KRUG

Füll mir den Krug,
den blauen mit weißen Tupfen,
gib ein wenig Trauer hinein,
ein Körnchen Schlaf
und ein Quentchen Liebe
und von der Sorge den Staub,
denn wir dürfen den Staub nicht vergessen!
Und stell ihn ins Fenster,
der Sonne am nächsten,
für einen honighellen Augenblick.

STILLEBEN

Streichhölzer, abgebrannt,
und Schuhe, die nicht gehen wollen,
Auslaufmodelle.
Die Gardine weht hell nach Westen.
Aus den Klöstern der Nacht
unklare Stimmen.
Wieder ein paar Worte weniger,
und der Mund wird schmaler,
wie schwer gekränkt.

GENEALOGIE

1
Auf der Lenzer Heide
habe ich eine Mücke erschlagen.
Eine ihrer Vorfahren begleitete
Nietzsche auf dem Weg ins Engadin.

2
Eine Kuh weidet vor dem Haus,
die letzte in einer Reihe von Kühen.
Eine ihrer Vorfahren, braun-weiß,
wurde Napoleon vorgelegt,
kurz bevor er Goethe in Weimar traf.

SPÄTE LEKTÜREN

Der Sturm reißt an den Läden,
als wolle er das Licht rauben,
das die Schrift mühsam hervorbringt,
mein Festland der Träume.
Ein Krieg, der zu lange dauert,
ist nicht zu gewinnen.
Er schläft irgendwann ein.
Dabei glaubten wir doch,
wir Ungläubigen, vom Himmel
sei nichts zu befürchten.
Die Kiefer, tagsüber aufrecht
wie ein Großinquisitor,
legt sich krumm und schreibt
ihr Geständnis ins Gras.
Anfällig sein. Anfällig bleiben
wie der bleiche Bach,
der sich ständig erneuert
in einer anderen Sprache.
Wäre es anders, wir hätten
das Paradies nicht verlassen müssen.

NACH DEM REGEN

Ein Hund zieht ein ängstliches Leben
über die Straße, ein Kind trägt seinen Gott
in einer Plastiktüte unter der Jacke,
die Krähen wollen wieder Theologen sein.
Erst nach dem Regen wird sich die Welt verändern.
Der Fluß rollt mir entgegen,
er schreit so laut, daß ich in ihm untergehe.
Die Zeichen der Bücher stehen auf Sturm,
nach dem Regen werden wir sie lesen,
wenn es ein Nach-dem-Regen geben sollte.

MEIN TALISMAN

Mein Talisman ist eine winzige Maus,
kleiner als gewöhnliche Mäuse.
Sie ißt, was ich esse. Sie ist aus Holz.
Tagsüber nagt sie an der Schönheit,
nachts an meinem Herzen.
Ihr Herz höre ich schlagen.
Wenn es wahr ist, daß man im Tod
alle früheren Gesichter zurückerhält,
wird mein letztes Gesicht an sie denken.

UNANGEMELDETER BESUCH

Es klingelt. Eine Frau bittet
um Münzen für die Augen
ihrer toten Tochter.
Ich gebe ihr zwei Nüsse
von meinen Nußbäumen,
von jedem Baum eine.
Dort, wo die Kronen sich treffen,
entsteht ein dichtes Tympanon,
in dessen Mitte die Amsel sitzt
mit ihrem olivfarbenen Augen.
Die Frau nimmt die Nüsse
und geht – und ich, in Panik,
laufe zurück zu meinem Buch
über den "unendlichen Raum",
um seine Sprache nicht zu verlernen.

KLEINE KIRCHE

Manchmal, in den kleinen Kirchen,
möchte man den Bildern danken,
daß sie dageblieben sind: Lazarus,
der aus dem Salpeter wächst
wie ein helles Geschwür, und Jonas,
der nicht weiß, wo er gelandet ist,
Heilige, die ihre Träume auftragen,
und Märtyrer ohne Kopf und ohne Kragen.
Es gibt keine Erlösung, flüstern sie,
aber ein zweites Leben gibt es auch für dich.
Schwalben verteilen ein Licht,
das sonst in die Dunkelheit fiele,
und von draußen hört man den Hahn.
Mehr kannst du nicht erwarten,
wenn du hinaustrittst in die glückliche Nacht.
Ein zweites Leben?
Nur keine Frömmigkeit aus Schwäche!
rufen die Bilder dir nach.

IM MOOR, IM MÄRZ

Wenn einen das Unglück am Wickel hat,
gibt es keinen Ort, der trostloser aussieht.
Die mickrigen Birken bilden einen Orden,
dem keiner beitreten will, und der Boden
stöhnt, als hätte er den Verstand verloren.
Was hier einsinkt, bleibt erhalten.
So stelle ich mir, Gefangener der Kindheit,
das Paradies vor, nach der Vertreibung.

HUND

Ich liebe schattige Wege
und den Park an der Ecke,
wo die Penner über Gott und die Welt reden.
Sie dürfen mich Hund nennen,
meinen bürgerlichen Namen habe ich
kürzlich verloren.
Mir gefällt's, wieder namenlos zu sein
zwischen Häusern und Menschen.
Gott, sagte kürzlich ein armes Schwein,
hat zu viele Namen vergeben,
jetzt kennt er sich selbst nicht mehr aus.
Hund.
Nur ich weiß, was sich dahinter verbirgt.

HOTELZIMMER

Als ich, noch im Mantel, mein Zimmer betrete,
ohne Hoffnung auf Einsicht und Schlaf,
sind schon, zur Begrüßung, alle Zimmer
versammelt, in denen ich einst schlief.
Die traurigen Tapeten, die Kunstgeschichte
von ihrer schlechtesten Seite, das Sofa,
in dessen Ritzen noch Romane leben.
Die lustlose Bibel, gebunden in Kunststoff,
mit Eselsohren an den schweren Stellen.
Und auch der ungerührte Spiegel,
der mich nicht erkennen will.
Vor der Tür stehen die Toten.
Sie tun nichts. Sie warten.
Sei nur ruhig, flüstern sie,
bald ist auch dieses Leben ausgestanden.

DIE SPINNE

Vor dem Haus spielen die Kinder
verrückt, als gäbe es nur
Freund oder Feind. Ich denke
an die grundlose Frömmigkeit,
unzugänglich dem Gebet.
Im Zimmerwinkel arbeitet
die Spinne an der Reinschrift der Natur.
Wenn sie ihr Netz gespannt hat,
ist die Kindheit zu Ende.

ÜBER GNADE

Das Wort Gnade ging
von Satz zu Satz und bat
vergeblich um Einlaß.
Gröbere und härtere Wörter
hatten die Stühle besetzt
und führten ein Stück auf,
das Wirklichkeit hieß,
eine Tragödie, ohne Pause
und mit großem Erfolg.
Ein Stück über einsame Wörter.

SAECULUM OBSCURUM

Riesige Wolken von Süden,
ein monumentales Volksbuch,
aus dem verwischte Schatten
auf die Erde fallen.
Alexander ließ seinen Kopf
auf harte Münzen prägen,
immer das eine Profil,
ein Eindruck von Wahrheit.
Im Wald übt man
die Vogelpredigt,
da gehören wir hin.

VORORTKNEIPE

Die Situation ist undurchsichtig,
zwei Neonröhren, die keinen Schatten werfen,
ein Kind dreht das Rad der Leere,
es hat mich durchschaut.
Der Kellner ist Araber. Er erzählt
die Geschichte von Mohammed,
der sich hinter einem Spinnennetz versteckte.
Es gibt nachtblaue Schnäpse,
die den Koran überlisten sollen.
Und dann ein Lied. Und alle stehen auf
und weinen.

TAGESSCHAU

Deutschland hat sein Geld verloren,
und wir sollen es, sagt der Sprecher,
wieder herbeischaffen, wenn auch
in drei Generationen. Außerdem
geht die Sonne unter um 19 Uhr 7.
Mord und Totschlag auf allen
fünf Erdteilen, die älteste Japanerin
hat sich von Acker gemacht
und die ganze Welt mitgenommen.
Um 19 Uhr 10 ist es stockdunkel.

TOD DES DICHTERS

Der unreiner Hof,
zwischen den Worten das Unkraut.
Der Wald dahinter zeigt sein zerfurchtes Profil.
Im Haus des Toten noch Licht,
im Fenster wütende Motten,
sie wollen Abschied nehmen.
Vor der Tür Briefe und Zeitungen,
sie melden, auf der ersten Seite,
den Tod des Dichters, damit die Ameisen
wissen, wer hier betrauert wird.

ÜBER KINDHEIT

Als die Kindheit zu Ende war,
hörte das Staunen auf.
Ich stand, es war doch erst gestern,
am Feldrand, wo Mohn und Kamille
mir Märchen erzählten,
und starrte, die Hand über den Augen,
der untergehenden Sonne nach.
In der Linde, alter als Krieg
und alter als Frieden,
hing der Bürgermeister und hörte,
kopfunter, den Bienen zu.
Er hatte es nicht so gewollt.

INS REINE

Wir haben meine Kindheit nachgestellt
mit unscheinbaren Dingen.
Einem Tannzapfen, Brotkrumen,
Schlüsseln, einem schwarzgeäderten Stein,
alles was zur Hand ist und beweglich.
Nur haben die Dinge die Neigung,
nach eignem Belieben zu handeln,
und die Bahn, die ich auslegen wollte,
neigt sich ständing vor und zurück.
Ich sehe das, was ich nicht mehr bin,
aber ich sehe nicht mich.
Ein Apfel rollt traurig vom Tisch
und bricht, wie Wörter brechen,
wenn man sie lang nicht benutzt.
Überlaß es den Vögeln, das Gekrakel
ins Reine zu schreiben, auf sie ist
Verlaß.

UMSTELLUNG DER ZEIT

WIE GEDICHTE ENTSTEHEN

Jeder kennt den Moment,
da man auf die Lichtung tritt
und die Hasen,
nach einer Sekunde des Zögerns,
im Unterholz verschwinden.
Es gibt kein Wort,
das sie aufhalten könnte.
Du bist wohl nicht bei Trost,
sagte mein Vater,
wenn mir die Tränen kamen.
Wie soll man ein Ganzes denken,
wenn man nicht weiß,
was ein Ganzes ist?

KRÄHENBEIßER

Krähen, erzählt einer,
der den Krieg überlebt hat,
muss man mit dem Holz
der Kiefer kochen,
das bindet die Gifte.
Und Sauerampfer dazu,
der von den Tieren verschmäht wird.
Unverständlich ist die Ordnung
der Welt im Frieden.
Wir sitzen im Freien und bestaunen
den Sonnenuntergang.
Die Krähen auf der Kiefer
haben das letzte Wort.

ICH WEIß NICHT, WAS SOLL ES BEDEUTEN

Im Wald habe ich Brombeeren gefunden,
eng verbandelt mit einem lammellenartig gestreiften Efeu,
der eine Ruine umklammerte, eine bröckelnde Wand,
an der eine Klingel hing. Sie war heiß von der Sonne.
Ich drückte den Klingelknopf, nur so zum Spaß.
Schon gingen ein paar Götter über die Lichtung.
leichten Schrittes und ins Gespräch vertieft,
und einer lief hinterdrein, der wollte für sich sein.
Was Götter so reden. Wenn nicht alles täuscht,
werden wir demnächst unser exaktes Todesdatum wissen,
hörte ich einen, es steht schon geschrieben.
Ich hatte verstanden, begreifen wollte ich nichts.

HOLZHAUS
für Alfred Kolleritsch

Mit dem Rücken zur Wand
muss man stehen, im Abendlicht.
Dann sieht man den Sturm,
wie er sich ankündigt in der Krone
der Linde. Die verrückten Amseln,
als ginge es um ein Spätwerk.
Man wird daran gemessen, wie oft
man die Wahrheit nicht gesagt hat,
obwohl das Wort warm auf der Zunge lag.
Ein Blick auf die rasenden Wolken,
und man versteht den Bruch
zwischen himmlischer und irdischer Welt.
Der Rücken am warmen Holz,
und dann der Sonnenuntergang.

GLÜCK

Wie die Lupinen riechen,
die Schafgarbe nach dem Regen,
der Knöterich, den der Stein
nicht hergeben will.
Es dauert zu lange,
bis man zurückgeschickt wird
in die Kindheit,
als die Worte Zeit hatten,
ihren Reichtum zu zeigen.
Eine späte Erkenntnis,
durch Schwäche gewonnen.
Würdest du mir jetzt
eine Saubohne zeigen,
ich würde tot umfallen
vor Glück.

DER LETZTE TAG IM AUGUST

Der Apfelbaum trägt schwer
an seiner Last, bald wird er
die Früchte ins Gras werfen,
weil ich sie nicht pflücke.
Es ist windstill, und dennoch
beginnt ein einzelnes Blatt
sich zu drehen wie irr.
Etwas stimmt nicht.
Auch die Vögel halten den Schnabel.
Was wir, nach langem Grübeln,
die Dichte des Lebens nennen,
stellt das Wort in Frage,
die Sprache versagt.
Die Dichte ist wortlos,
und jetzt liegt der Apfel beim Stamm.

DER TOD DER BIRKE, 2011

Zuerst wuchs ihr ein Pilz
aus der Hüfte, ein fetter Schwamm,
dann nahm ihr ein Wind die Blätter
und ließ sie achtlos sinken,
zuletzt verlor sie die Farbe.
So stelle ich mir den Abschied vor,
die kleinen Untergänge vor der Zeit.
Heute knickte sie ein.
Der Stein, der ihren Fuß bewachte,
läßt sich nicht aus der Fassung bringen.
Eine neue Zeitrechnung beginnt,
das Jahr eins nach dem Tod der Birke.

ERINNERUNG AN DIE SCHULE

Eine sprach nur von Akazien,
sie war verrückt nach ihrem Duft.
Plinius kannte sie auswendig,
Horaz lag ihr am Herzen,
Boetius war ihr ein Gott.
Aber wenn die Akazien blühten,
war sie nicht mehr zu halten.
Ihr Name fällt mir nicht ein.

GEDICHT

Ich könnte von Kriegen erzählen,
von Göttern, die sich aus Langeweile
das Leben ausdachten, von Igeln
in meinem Garten, von mir.
Ich könnte von einem Mann erzählen,
der die Lesarten des Unglücks studiert
wie ein rumänischer Philosoph.
Auch mit Lorbeer
kann man Dämonen vertreiben.
Aber lieber die Klappe halten,
die Stille ist laut genug.

IM NEGEV

für N. C.

Ich habe den Bären gesehen,
wie er den Schild des Feindes umarmt,
und den Löwen, der im Schatten
der Tamariske das Rind erlegt.
Die Jagd als schmackhaftes Wissen.
Ich habe den Sand gezählt
im Negev, den herrlichen Sand,
der meine Spur nicht halten kann.

HOTEL BEI ERFURT

Nur Tote wohnen hier,
sie bezahlen mit Asche.
Ihre Schatten sieht man
hinter den Fenstern,
auch die Schatten von Kindern.
Der Taxifahrer erzählte
von einem Mathematiker
aus Jena, '45 gestorben,
der wußte die genaue Zahl
aller Toten auf Erden.
Keiner geht verloren.
Man darf kein Gepäck haben,
wenn man hier einziehen will.
Sogar Bücher sind verboten.

ERLEUCHTUNG

Wie ich so stehe,
gibt mir das Meer
ein Licht,
das mich entzündet, und mit den Füßen
lese ich
die Blindenschrift der Kiesel.

266

SCHAM

Mailicht. Spät kam einer vorbei,
schälte sich aus dem Dunkel der Hecke
und sprach in der kindlichen Sprache
der Zweige. Bäuerlich sah er aus,
die Mütze hing ihm tief in die Stirn.
Den Fledermäusen war er treu,
er lobte den Katechismus der Tiere,
aber seine Liebe galt den Clownereien
der Schmetterlinge vor dem Kältetod.
Wir saßen auf der Bank vor dem Haus,
schauten dem Tropfen zu,
wie er sich endlich füllt und fällt.
Er ging dann weiter, der späte Erzähler,
nur seinen Namen ließ er zurück,
einen unaussprechlichen Namen.
All seine Erzählungen hätte auch ich
erzählen können, dachte ich,
aber ich habe geschwiegen aus Scham.

ZIMT

Plötzlich kommt einer auf Zimt,
als sei das die Erklärung
für alle geheimen Verstrickungen
zwischen Himmel und Erde: Zimt.
Meine Großmutter hatte vier Stangen
über den Krieg gerettet, mehr nicht.
Die Birke schüttelt den Winter ab,
der Wind prüft ihre Standfestigkeit.
Und ich denke nur an Zimt.
Von mir aus darf man
den Mond einen Kürbis nennen,
aber wenn einer Zimt sagt,
spüre ich nichts als die Wärme der Toten.

GESCHENKTE ZEIT

Das Taxi kommt zu spät, der Bus
kann nicht warten, und das Flugzeug
weigert sich, aus technischen Gründen,
den festen Boden zu verlassen. Du weißt,
wie das ist, eine Leere im Magen,
tief, fest und finster,
geschenkte Zeit. Öffentliche Telefonzellen,
das war gestern. Ich hätte auch nicht
gewußt, wie ich es hätte erklären sollen.
So viele Worte, die man nur sagt,
um sie loszuwerden. Raus damit!
Vor dir wimmeln fremde Taxis und Busse,
über dir kreuzen Flugzeuge, ihre Schleier
driften dahin in die Gegend, wo
deine Erzählung ankommen wollte.
Die Hälfte des Himmels in Brand.
Ein Anfang, der keinen Anfang hat,
und ein Ende ohne Ende, und ein Blitz,
der die Zeit zerreißt wie altes Papier.

ISTANBUL REVISITED
für Sezer Duru

Nach dreißig Jahren besuchte ich wieder
die Karpfen in der Zisterne von Istanbul.
Damals brannte ein Öltanker im Bosporus,
der den Namen "Independenta" trug.
Wie eine rostige Schildkröte schnappte
er nach Luft, um das Feuer anzuheizen,
und junge anatolische Soldaten
mußten mit Schnellfeuergewehren
den Rauch vertreiben, der schwarz über der Stadt
hing und uns die Sprache verschlug.
Ich sehe noch die dicken Wülste der Kabel
über den Straßen, gespickt mit Krähen,
die im Auftrag des Geheimdienstes
das Flüstern abhörten über Hammelfleischpreise,
Liebe und die Arbeit in Deutschland.
Die Eule rief von Afrasiabs Türmen die Stunde aus,
und die Spinne webte die Vorhänge im Palast der Cäsaren.
Jetzt sah ich auch die Karpfen wieder in der Zisterne
von Istanbul, seit Justinian geben sie Auskunft
über das Schicksal des Reiches.
Mit der Leidenschaft schwerer Tiere ziehen sie
die Schwermut über die bemoosten Steine,
meine uralten Brüder, die alles wissen,
und doch nicht handeln, sie blicken nicht einmal auf,
wenn eine Münze sie trifft aus Europa.
Manche liegen, trostlos und dunkel, wie Intarsien
am Grund und lesen gründelnd
die *historia arcana* über den Einfall der Barbaren.
Was sie rettet, ist der Mangel an Licht.

DIEL

Die Butterbirne
geht auf sein Konto,
den leberroten Himbeerapfel
hat er nach Form und Geschmack
genauer beschrieben
als die Kunsthistoriker
das Obst auf holländischen Bildern.
Farbe und Textur des Fleisches,
Standort und Kultur des Bodens,
die große englische Renette
ließ ihn lange nicht los.
Alles wurde erforscht,
nur die Systematik der Obstbäume
fand vor ihm keinen Homer.
Mein Apfelbaum
trägt wieder Früchte, und alle
sind ungenießbar und schön.

CZESŁAW MIŁOSZ

Das Jahr hatte so gut begonnen.
Ich durfte den heiligen Rochus besuchen,
der die Tiere heilte, während am anderen Ende
der Straße Bürgerkriege ausbrachten
und ihr Blut über den Bildschirm suppte.
Die winzige Pforte der Erinnerung,
lange verschlossen, ging plötzlich auf,
und ich sah mich mitten in Venedig,
auf einer Bank sitzen, die für den Tod
reserviert war. Frauen gingen vorbei,
die geheime Botschaften flüsterten
auf dem Weg zum Bahnhof oder zum Boot,
und dann kam Miłosz auf mich zu,
den Spazierstock im Rücken, ein Netz
in der Hand mit glitzernden Fischen.
Man sah ihm den Tod nicht an,
wie er so dastand und Gedichte aufsagte,
wie andere von gestiegenen Preisen reden
für Wahrheit, für Obst und Gemüse.

WAS NOCH ZU TUN IST

für Peter Handke zum 70. Geburtstag

Die Nüsse einsammeln,
bevor der Eichkatz sie holt;
den Schatten in Sicherheit bringen;
mit dem Bleistift reden,
wenn er die Worte verweigert;
den Feind nicht finden wollen,
der im Ungedachten brütet;
in den Wolken lesen,
dem unabschließbaren Epos
über Form und Verwandlung;
den Stein von der Stirn heben;
dem Staunen eine Gnadenfrist geben.

Und nicht vergessen: den Ort aufsuchen,
wo sich das Buch versteckt hält,
das Buch mit den leeren Seiten,
das leere Buch, das Buch.

CLAUDE SIMON

Im Traum setzte sich
Claude Simon neben mich,
ganz grün im Gesicht.
Er hatte, aus Versehen,
Bouletten gegessen,
am Wannsee in Berlin.
An seinen kleinen Händen
zog ich ihn zurück
ins wirkliche Leben.
Wir tranken seinen Wein,
einen provençalischen Roten,
und lasen die Georgica,
die er neu schreiben wollte
nach dem Krieg.
"Verzicht auf Verwirklichung",
viel mehr sagte er nicht,
Sprechen war nicht seine Stärke.
"Sehen Sie den Schmetterling?"
sagte er zum Abschied,
"Odysseus, der nicht heimkehren will."
Da wachte ich auf.

WER WAR ES?

Im Honig vom vergangenen Jahr
steckt unversehrt
eine Fliege.
Der perfekte Mord.
Kriminalromane
könnten so anfangen
oder so enden.

ARME ÄPFEL IM FEBRUAR

Noch hängen Äpfel an den kahlen Ästen,
die hat der Frost verschont, als er,
von Süden kommend, über Nacht
mit einem rauhen Biß das Land versiegelte,
den Garten und den Blick in diesen Garten
und auch das Herz, das sich den Schnee erträumte.
Und was für Äpfel! Aufgeplatzte Schalen
und braunes, angefressenes Fleisch,
das selbst den Amseln nicht mehr schmeckt.
Entsetzlich, traurig: Als sei der Krieg,
der sich fürs Frühjahr angemeldet hatte,
jetzt schon durchgezogen.
Ich stand und schaute, bis ich nichts mehr sah,
was sich mit diesen armen Äpfeln messen konnte.

SETZLINGE

Heute wurden unsere zwei Agaven
zurückgebracht, die den Winter über
in einer Gärtnerei um die Ecke
in Pension waren, in einem Treibhaus
zusammen mit vornehmen Pflanzen,
wie sie in unserem Viertel geschätzt werden.
Ich dachte, sie hätten geschlafen
und von Mexiko geträumt oder der Levante,
von müden Eseln und der Stille,
nachdem die Bomben eingeschlagen haben.
Das Gegenteil ist der Fall.
Unter ihren gurkengrünen fleischigen Degen
schauen mehr als zwanzig Setzlinge hervor,
sorglos und neugierig wir junge Katzen.
Entfernen? fragt mich der Gärtner,
der nach nasser Wolle riecht.
Entweder sie werden den Tontopf sprengen
oder alle zusammen eingehen.
Ich bin jetzt achtundsehzig Jahre alt
und kann mich nicht mehr entscheiden.
Ende Oktober wissen wir mehr.

BEI BOSTON, AM MEER

Der Wind, müde der dornigen Hecken,
hat sich endlich gelegt –
Sei du auch jetzt still, Meer!
Der Morgen wie kalte Ashe.
Selbst die Insekten verzichten
auf ihr heidnisches Handiwerk.
Das Atmen kommt einem
wie eine Erfindung vor,
die man noch nicht beherrscht.
Von Gott ist nicht viel
zu sehen bei diesem Licht.

AN DER OSTSEE, SEHR FRÜH

I

Unruhig, wie die trippligen Strandläufer,
die am Morgen ihre Spur suchen
vom vergangenen Tag.
Wie Gräser, die keinen Schatten werfen.

Kinder, müde vom Schlaf,
knurren das Meer an.

Es hat lange gedauert,
bis die Botschaft des Kaisers
endlich angespült wude.
Aber jetzt will sie keiner wissen.

2

Leere Schneckenhäuser, Muscheln.
Das Gute sieht besser aus, als es ist,
das Böse wie immer zu wortreich.

POSTKARTE, MAI 2012

Die Tür zur Terasse steht offen,
die gelbe Armee des gemeinen Löwenzahns
erobert unerbittlich den Rasen,
das Eichhörnchen sucht die Nüsse
vom letzten Jahr. Es soll regnen,
die Schaukel träumt schon vom Wind.
Wenn die dicken Sonntagszeitungen
recht haben, gibt es das alles nicht.
Den Specht nicht, der seine Elegie
dem Ahorn anvertraut, und nicht
das Unkraut, den Freund der Hummeln.
Weil wir die Unvollkommenheit verachten,
arbeitet jetzt eine unsichtbare Maschine
an der Vollkommentheit. Übrigens,
auch der Apfelbaum, der wie ich
im Krieg das Licht der Welt erblickt hat,
beginnt wieder zu blühen.

LICHTUNG

1

Das Drama der Blätter,
wenn sie fallen; und du,
weit weg, bemühst dich,
eine Welt zu lesen, wo keiner
das Lebewohl mehr versteht,
die Umkehr auf halben Weg
zwischen Auge und Herz.

2

Blätter beweinen die Toten,
nur die Spatzen, unbekümmert,
lassen sich abspeisen mit Krümeln.
Die kommende Welt,
durchs böse Auge gesehen,
nimmt ihren Anfang
im hilfsbereiten Herz der Wörter.

3

Alles zittert.
Und God zittert auch.

Biographical Note

Michael Krüger published his first collection of poems, *Reginapoly*, in 1976. His works include: *Diderots Katze* (Hanser Verlag, 1978), *Das Ende des Romans. Eine Novelle* (Residenz Verlag, 1990), *Nachts, unter Bäumen* (Residenz Verlag, 1996), *Die Cellospielerin* (Suhrkamp Verlag, 2000), *Scenes from the Life of a Bestselling Author* (Harvill, 2002), *Das Falsche Haus: Eine Novelle* (Suhrkamp, 2002), *Kurz vor dem Gewitter* (Suhrkamp Verlag, 2003), *Unter freiem Himmel* (Suhrkamp Verlag, 2007), *Die Turiner Komoedie Bericht eines Nachlassverwalters* (Suhrkamp Verlag, 2007), *Ins Reine* (Suhrkamp Verlag, 2010), and *Umstellung der Zeit* (Suhrkamp Verlag, 2013).

Krüger was publisher and editor at Hanser Verlag for 45 years until his retirement in 2013, when he was presented the Lifetime Achievement Award in International Publishing at the London Book Fair. He won the 1986 Toucan Prize, and in 1996, the Prix Médicis étranger. He is also editor of the literary magazine *Akzente*.

About the Translators

Karen Leeder is Professor of Modern German Literature at Oxford's New College. She has translated from the German, Evelyn Schlag, Raoul Schrott, Durs Grünbein, and Volker Braun. She won the Schegel-Tieck Prize in 2005 for her translation of Evelyn Schlag's *Selected Poems* (Carcanet, 2004) and the Times Stephen Spender Prize for her translation of Durs Grünbein in 2013. Her translation of Michael Krüger's *Scenes from the Life of a Best-Selling Author* was published by Harvill in 2002.

Richard Dove was born in 1954 in Bath. He is a distinguished poet and translator. He read Modern Languages at Oxford and lectured at various English universities before moving to Munich in 1987. His work includes *From an Earlier Life: Poems English / German* (Lyrikedition, 2000).

INDEX

278

281

282